10 Ways to Future-Proof Yourself, Fearlessly Innovate, and Succeed Despite Uncertainty

MAKE CHANGE WORK FOR YOU

SCOTT STEINBERG

A NEW BLUEPRINT FOR SUCCESS IN AN INCREASINGLY UNCERTAIN WORLD.

FEATURES:

- 10 new success skills that can ignite your business, brand or career
- A revolutionary new system for future-proofing yourself in an increasingly uncertain world
- Practical, proven strategies for unleashing your creativity and innovation
- A simple, four-part formula for creating competitive advantage
- How to overcome the one thing holding most of us back from success

www.MakeChangeWorkForYou.com

CREATE VALUE. STAY AHEAD OF THE CURVE.

SCOTT STEINBERG

KEYNOTE SPEAKER | STRATEGIC CONSULTANT
BESTSELLING AUTHOR | TECHNOLOGY FUTURIST

AS SEEN IN:

ENGAGE, INNOVATE AND BECOME INVALUABLE

ACCELERATE GROWTH AND TRANSFORMATION THROUGH STRATEGIC INNOVATION AND COMPETITIVE ADVANTAGE

#1-RANKED BUSINESS STRATEGIST, TECHNOLOGY AND TREND FORECASTER

- World-famous for 10+ years of accurately predicting business, consumer and technology trends
- Bestselling author featured in 600+ outlets from NPR to USA Today
- Google's #1-ranked technology expert — seen by 1 billion+ worldwide
- Strategic advisor to Fortune 500 businesses and brands
- Expert columnist on change and innovation for CNN, Rolling Stone and The Huffington Post
- Noted entrepreneur who's built and sold startups and divisions

SPEAKING TOPICS

- » Business
- » Leadership
- » Management
- » Marketing
- » Sales
- » Social Media
- » Communication
- » Education
- » Healthcare
- » Technology
- » Teamwork
- » Customer Service

10 Ways to Future-Proof Yourself,
Fearlessly Innovate, and Succeed
Despite Uncertainty

**MAKE
CHANGE WORK
FOR YOU**

TO BOOK SCOTT PLEASE CONTACT:

Perceptive Research LLC | info@akeynotespeaker.com | 888-507-2246
www.AKeynoteSpeaker.com

The Modern Parent's Guide to
FACEBOOK AND SOCIAL NETWORKS

To order copies or to request permission to reprint, contact the publisher at:
Published by READ.ME and TechSavvy Global LLC

www.AKeynoteSpeaker.com
www.TechSavvyGlobal.com

DEDICATION

For Z, and to modern families, educators and advocates for
today's youth worldwide – may it guide and serve you well.

INTRODUCTION

Believe it or not, social networks aren't a new phenomenon. Researchers in Europe have suggested that ancient tribes would actually seek out and update rock art in common locations in places like Russia and Sweden, adding content each season that they would visit. Whether it was the latest news on what animals to hunt or where plentiful sources of shelter could be found, the information they were sharing was valuable enough for them to keep returning generation after generation, sharing knowledge each time they passed through.Eventually, scientists say, these prehistoric humans would even copy the rock art onto smaller stones so they could take it with them as they set off to new locations – meaning that even cavemen were using a form of mobile social networking!

Although it might seem strange to think of Neanderthals using social networks, consider that at a basic level, the practice of sharing drawings, words, pictures, symbols or any other form of communications that captures one's thoughts or experiences with others is essentially the same system found at the heart of today's online social platforms. Granted, the methods and mechanisms of social networking have evolved over the years, leading us to today's infinitely more high-tech era of 24/7 connectivity wherein interaction can occur across a spectrum of portable or stationary electronic devices. Nowadays, of course, kids and families can access online social networks nearly anytime, anywhere in order to share what they're doing, where they're hanging out, and how they feel with friends and loved ones, and even immediately and very publicly Interact with acquaintances, celebrities and even total strangers in the time it takes to prod a touchscreen. But despite the marked differences in social communications platforms and how we interact with them that have evolved over the centuries, some commonalities remain.

Case in point: Whether you're discussing Facebook, Twitter, Instagram or other online services, a social network effectively serves as a dedicated system or space designed to facilitate communications and user Interaction. Likewise, members are further encouraged to create and share content of all kinds designed for enjoyment and consumption by others in their sphere of connectivity. Although the underlying infrastructure is provided by the service itself (and is constantly changing and updating), the content shared within it – i.e. status updates, tweets, photos, videos and article links – is all shared specifically by people or organizations you are connected to. Happily, you can also provide similar information to others linked to you in like fashion.

Here's why these points are important to note: At their heart, social networks fundamentally require that sizable groups of people be using and contributing to them in order to function and thrive, and grow in potential interest and impact with every additional member who participates. It's the reason why platforms like Facebook continue to be so popular, and why services like MySpace have evolved into more niche offerings. At this point, amongst younger generations especially, it's almost more common for someone to be a social network user than not. And the statistics surrounding their popularity are so large that numbers are almost difficult to comprehend. Facebook now boasts more than 1.44 billion users worldwide, Twitter has more than 302 million active users, and most major services keep growing with each passing day.

While not all individuals with registered accounts regularly use these solutions, the ones that are engaged use them frequently. Every day, there are more than three billion likes and comments on Facebook, and more than 350 million photos uploaded. Facebook averages 1.44 billion active users a month, each spending an average of 21 minutes on the service per day. Even though more than half of Twitter accounts are potentially inactive as well, there are still more than 500 million tweets per day.

What's more, other social networking sites continue to emerge and blossom on a frequent basis, i.e. Pinterest, which became the fastest site ever to hit 10 million monthly visitors back in 2012. Today, Pinterest has nearly 73 million users, sending out 2 million pins every day.

All of the sharing we do is united under a single virtual identity that provides personal representation, often taking the form of an account name, photo or image, and frequently referred to as an avatar, which is used to represent our online presence. Granted, names and categorizations differ by service: On Facebook, posts are usually found under the banner of an account bearing your name and photo, while Twitter users can go by any nickname or handle they want, and other social networks, especially those geared towards kids, actually encourage users to use made-up titles or cartoon images (CoolKid78) rather than post their real likeness and name. In all cases though, avatars or personalized profiles are a primary feature of social networks. Each user bears a distinct online identity, and they're then free to use that identity to connect with others under its banner, often sharing content such as messages, status updates, photos, videos or online links. Social network users can share both content that they themselves have created, or share access to or comment on content that others have built.

Needless to say, the way the world gets its information is evolving, and social networks are at the forefront. Announcements now break on Twitter, and rumors fly at the speed of Facebook. Whether it's word of political uprising, the emergence of an unexpected earthquake or even a celebrity scandal, many people now get their first taste of news from social networking sites, and then visit traditional news and media websites to read more about it. On the social network Reddit, which many kids use, an 18 year-old user quickly compiled updates garnered throughout the night during the tragic theater shooting in Aurora, CO, and was reporting the information gathered thereby before any news website or telecast had it, thanks to deft use of social media updates.

Because of social network sites, many notable individuals and organizations – including celebrities, news media, major corporations and public figures – now use social media as a platform to directly connect with followers and the public at large. Social networks' power to influence policy and impact history can't be denied either. Issues like the Trayvon Martin case were at first dismissed by public officials, but after continuous tweets, Facebook posts and other messages demanding action from the general public, law enforcement officialswere forced to investigate, eventually arresting George Zimmerman. During the 2012 Election, President Obama actually participated in an "AMA"

(Ask Me Anything) chat on Reddit, which quickly crashed the company's servers, while also providing mainstream media attention to a service that's every bit as much a part of kids' lives as more well-known platforms like Facebook, Instagram and Twitter.

Curiously though, it's worth noting, even these near-ubiquitous social networks are viewed differently by kids and adults. Adults use social networks like Facebook to stay connected or reconnect with old friends, and share updates on life events. But kids use social networks in a more unique fashion. Generation Tech, as we refer to them – children born into the connected era – have never known a world without Facebook, and they're compelled to be connected to anyone and everyone in their class or school. The information they choose to share is therefore vastly different than the kind adults might, and often seemingly more mundane. Ask yourself: Would members of our generation really want to tell our entire 11th grade class about our trip to the local pizza place? Unlikely – but today's kids may feel compelled, and see the revelation actually prompt a seemingly random and lively conversation about what kind of toppings everybody likes.

Also worth keeping in mind: The way that kids can connect is different on each social network. Some services require actions to be taken by both parties in order for them to be connected, which is one reason why many parents seem to trust Facebook – both individuals must agree to be connected in order to see each other's updates. (Unless, of course, your privacy settings aren't configured correctly, but we'll discuss that more in a bit...) But others social networks like Twitter may require users to merely click on a public "follow" button to gain consistent access to all information that a party is sharing without the need for said party's approval. That's why Twitter is a useful way to keep tabs on your favorite celebs, sports stars or other well-known individuals, but why it's not the best platform to communicate with those you're seeking to engage in more private exchanges with.

The simple fact that kids are "on" social networks isn't necessarily anything to be concerned with (unless you're exceptionally paranoid.) More important to consider are topics such as who they're interacting with, how, when, and what it is they're up to online – especially in shared company. Unfortunately, examples of what not to do on social networks seem all too common. Whether it's posting inappropriate videos, uploading an abundance of pictures with alcohol prominently involved throughout them, or sharing generally distasteful updates, schools and employers are increasingly keeping an eye on what students and employees are doing, and reacting accordingly. Moreover, there are also some potentially grave consequences to misuse and abuse of social networks. Consider the case of Tyler Clementi, a homosexual teen who tragically committed suicide after his roommate posted videos of his sexual encounters on Twitter.

However, as a parent or caregiver, you shouldn't be scared off by many of the stories you hear in the media. Like any other form of technology, social networks are simply a neutral tool for communication and engagement – whether you have a positive or negative experience is all in how they're used. Each and every individual's social network experience will be completely unique, because it's the actions you engage in and contacts you interact with within your social network that help define one's takeaways. Chances are significantly greater than not that you and your kids will greatly enjoy the interaction and connections made possible by social networks, including the many friendships and relationships that these services enable that would never otherwise be possible in real life due to geographic or cultural limitations.

In addition, many parents may not realize that Facebook's terms of service actually require users to be at least 13 years of age before they can receive an account. The main reason for this is because of the laws in place that restrict marketing and collecting data about kids under this age, which fall under the Children's Online Privacy Protection Act (COPPA). However, recent estimates place the number of preteen children using the service in violation of its policies as high as 7.5 million in the U.S. alone, according to Consumer Reports. More than 5 million of these tots are just 10 and under. Many parents are even actively lying to help underage kids join the service, according to top experts. As a result, Facebook itself is exploring ways to make its content accessible to a wide variety of individuals and age groups while also maintaining compliance with privacy laws.

While the vast majority of online interactions are positive in nature, the fact that so many kids are now on social networks also means though that there's a pressing responsibility for parents, teachers, law enforcement officials and even companies themselves to promote greater public education and awareness. Believe it or not, service providers such as Facebook, Twitter and Google all take their responsibilities with regard to safekeeping children very seriously, even though it's become common for users to gripe about seemingly constant redesigns and switches to these providers' privacy and information sharing policies. For example, Facebook has a number of initiatives geared towards educating and informing teens and kids using their site, whether it's the tips available in the company's Family Safety Center or through initiatives such as partnering with Trend Micro for the annual "What's Your Story" video contest to help build awareness for and prevent issues such as cyberbullying, sexting and other rising concerns. However, the responsibility for keeping children safe is one we all must share — only by working together can we ensure that kids enjoy a secure and beneficial online experience.

In essence, social networks today provide a core framework and infrastructure for online communication, just as streets and highways act as a form of infrastructure that allows for inter- and intrastate commerce. While few highways in and of themselves can cause danger, when populated with cars of all shapes and sizes, each traveling at different speeds towards different destinations, well... It's no wonder you need to make sure you know what you're doing, where you're headed, and how to proceed with caution when traveling them, including having the good sense to both keep your eyes on the road, and buckle up and wear a safety belt.

When kids ride in cars, the law says that they must have additional protection in the form of car seats or boosters, and they must stay safely ensconced in these protective accessories until they reach a certain age. Alas, there's no such equivalent on the Internet, as parents are free to set their kids loose in the most public of spaces whenever they choose, sans safety precautions. Certainly, there are laws like COPPA which help restrict the amount of information that sites can collect and use about young children.

But ultimately it's up to parents to decide what their kids can and can't do online, and adequately prepare them to make smart decisions and practice safe computing habits. Allowing kids on social networks for the first time has in many ways become a major rite of passage, yet the only real equivalents for road safety items like car seats, seat belts and air bags that we can provide children on social networks are training, insight and knowledge. A parent who understands these services, how they can be used, and best practices for employing them, as well as what their kids are doing online, how, when, and whom with, has the best chance of keeping them safe.

Consider the following volume, a comprehensive guide to Facebook and other popular social networks, as a key way to arm yourself with the knowledge and facts about social media services that you'll need to keep your family safe going forward, and help them enjoy a positive and enjoyable online experience. Simply the starting point in what should be a long, comprehensive, and ongoing discussion amongst kids and adults alike, it provides the tools, tips and training you and your loved ones need to enjoy a long and prosperous relationship with social media. We sincerely hope it proves a boon to your household, and invite you to join in further discussions surrounding the topic at www.AKeynoteSpeaker.com – your contributions and insights are vital to keeping today's family better informed about the opportunities and challenges that social networks present.

THE BENEFITS OF SOCIAL NETWORKS

Social networks are now an important part of your child's development. A recent clinical report from the American Academy of Pediatrics entitled "The Impact of Social Media on Children, Adolescents and Families" found that a large part of this generation's social and emotional growth occurs while using social networks. The report listed a number of benefits for kids from being connected, such as better engagement with friends, family and community; enhanced learning opportunities via collaboration; connections with like-minded teens; and enhancement of creativity. Tellingly, the study also found that 22% of teenagers log onto their favorite social media sites more than 10 times a day.

Interestingly, other research has shown that social networks can provide marked health benefits, like improved memory retention and even help patients with issues like recovering from a stroke. Social media is also viewed by many as a great equalizer, allowing even low-income households to become more tech-savvy and connected to their community, thanks to their participation in digital dialogue and the sharing and uploading of media via a method and format that even those with limited prior exposure to technology can enjoy. Brain researchers from Rutgers University likewise recently noted how the issue of social media is affecting the brains of young kids in a news release featuring research and opinions from some of the leading minds in neuroscience. While considering whether social media is a driving force controlling our brain's development or vice versa, these experts noted that about all that they can say for certain is that social media is now firmly entrenched in our society, and that kids these days really have no choice as to whether or not to be influenced by it. In other words, when it comes to emotional/social growth and development, and the ability for this form of media to influence viewers' opinions, social networks clearly have a lasting impact.

Because social networks are bigger than ever (and continuing to grow in popularity), they are now an integral part of our culture. Whether used for dissemination of news and information, job prospecting or simply connecting with friends, it's practically unavoidable now for your family and kids to not be engaged on some level on social network sites. While it's easy to focus on the scary stuff when it comes to anything online – i.e. dangers such as cyberbullies, sexual predators or identity thieves – it's an unwise point of reference from which to begin viewing the topic of social media. As with other high–tech subjects, it's important you're not approaching social networks from the basis of fear. Yes: Dangers do exist, and we'll prepare you to address and deftly handle many of the challenges that can and may happen surrounding social media services in upcoming chapters. But it's more important that you start by gaining a firm understanding of why utilizing social networks is so crucial, and the power these platforms have to be a force for good in children's lives.

Parent safety resource ConnectSafely.org identifies a number of reasons why kids like to use Facebook and other social networks as part of its extremely helpful range of resources. Despite patent differences in consumption and communications habits, the site says that kids use these services for many of the same reasons adults do. According to their experts, social networks are great for:

• Hanging out and socializing with friends
• Keeping up with day to day news
• Schoolwork collaboration
• Self-expression and identity exploration
• Connecting with support systems
• Discovering and exploring interests
• Civic engagement in meaningful causes

When people think of kids and online interaction, they often default to picturing "nightmare scenarios," as David Cooper Moore from Temple University's Center for Media and Information Literacy recently told Newsworks.org. "If we focus only on the real risks that young people take online," Cooper says, "we may miss the complex ways that they are shaping their identities, extending their friendships, and finding new networks of support." In fact, there are a number of intriguing and positive reasons why kids are using social networks, and you may wish to encourage further usage. Let's take a closer look at a few of them.

Educational Benefits – Researchers in the field of connected learning point to social networks as a way for kids who have an interest in certain fields or subjects to receive support and information about subjects they are deeply passionate about. According to Dr. Mizuko Ito, a professor at UC-Irvine and cultural anthropologist of technology use, examples of connected learning occur when a teacher may ask a student to create a report on their favorite video game, or if a kid who likes to sew is able to make all the costumes for a school performance using information and ideas gained online.

Ito has found that kids benefit greatly and learn more when they associate online interactions with activities they already love. Social networks, says Ito, can "make this kind of learning accessible and ubiquitous. The power of digital networks is in the ability to connect learners and teachers across space and institutional boundaries, to build linkages between schools, homes and communities, and to make information and learning resources highly accessible and personalized." Ito says that kids interacting online are learning the skills necessary to participate in modern society. "Spending time online is essential for young people to pick up the social and technical skills they need to be competent citizens in the digital age."

Career and Job Insights – Now, more than ever, kids have a chance to connect and learn about areas of interest thanks to social networks. They can follow scientists, engineers, programmers, celebrities and news outlets, and easily access relevant links and trends simply by logging onto to a social network account. Likewise, they can quickly and effortlessly connect and communicate with potential peers, mentors and employers.

The flip side to the benefits of social networks as a tool for honing expertise in an area of interest or enhancing professional networking efforts is that any future potential employer can likely access any information shared, or any interaction that happened, on a social network: Kids need to be cognizant of the information and content that they share, and manner in which they comport themselves. But while it's easy to focus on negative potential consequences of youthful mistakes make online, there's an equally large

opportunity to for kids to show their knowledge and grasp of subjects. Such vehicles also make an excellent way to showcase their accomplishments or raise awareness for causes, whether promoting opportunities to contribute to the local food bank or letting others know they've finished first in a local debate contest.

Heightened Social Awareness – Although there's a perception among many that social networks consist solely of a bunch of people saying the digital equivalent of "Hey – look at me!" research shows that nearly half of all teens who use Facebook are more cause-oriented because of social networks. Actions they take here can be as simple as liking a charity or following these organizations on Facebook, but just as often, kids are at the forefront of spreading and disseminating videos and information that have a global focus and positive impact on society.

While many adults are critical of social networks, fearing that they are breeding a new generation of self-centered and spoiled brats, a recent study from World Vision actually showed that social media is opening teens' eyes and increasing their engagement with many charitable causes. Nearly half of all girls on social networks are apt to "like" or "follow" charities' pages and accounts, while just less than a third of boys do the same. Since 2006, the MacArthur Foundation has also explored the ways that digital media affects the way young people learn, communicate and play. A recent survey from the Foundation's Research Network on Youth and Participatory Politics found that social media services are playing a "crucial role" in the trend of 15-25 year olds participating in civic life. This observation is particularly interesting because by traditional standards, this group is judged to be the least involved in participatory politics. What this information shows is that, as parents, we need to rethink the ways that social media and social networks are influencing the way our kids live their lives.

Children are also directly impacting the world around them in very tangible form thanks to their participation on these services, with kids increasingly using social networks to kick-start their own funding campaigns and causes. A college student was able to raise more than $150,000 in relief funds for Haiti by simply creating an event on Facebook asking for donations and sharing it with friends and family. And a seven year-old boy in the UK named Charlie Simpson organized a 5-mile bike to raise more than $80,000 for the same cause.

Strengthened Relationships – There's benefit to both family and friendship relationships from social networks. Instead of seeing the cousins from Oregon once every two years at the family reunion, kids can now keep in constant contact with relatives, seeing photos or updates throughout the year. Grandma and Grandpa can now all know about the family trip to Sea World, or the doctor's office, with a simple status update as well.

Moreover, while kids often use social networks to strengthen their real-life relationships with friends, they don't see it as a replacement for face-to-face interaction. According to the "Children and Electronic Media" report for Princeton and the Brookings Institution, kids use social networking sites to keep in contact with their peers from their offline lives, both to make plans with friends whom they see often and to keep in touch with friends whom they see rarely.

Social networks can also give kids the confidence that can only come from interacting and socializing with friends. There are many opportunities in everyday life to receive positive reinforcement and feedback from adults such as parents, teacher and coaches, but social networks help kids collaborate, interact with and feel empowered by their peers.

Heightened Access to Information – Gone are the days of gathering around the boob tube for the six o'clock news. Instead, more often than not, everyone in the family seeks out information and forms their connections to the outside world through the lens of smartphones, tablets and laptops. Many families only watch on-demand content or media pre-recorded on digital video recorders (DVRs) on their TV these days as well – many times, social networks are one of a few select conduits where they still enjoy access to unfiltered information coming in from the outside world. (Albeit information that may be colored by the sharer's perspective or opinion.)

Whenever there's a big political development, natural disaster, court ruling or other major current event, many kids and adults often find out about it via social networks first. Consider that in numerous surveys about the method in which people found out about Osama bin Laden's demise in 2011, nearly half of all respondents in poll after poll cited social networks as their primary source of information – more than television or even text messaging. Likewise, in 2009, the US government actually asked Twitter to delay some scheduled maintenance as it would have occurred during a peak time for Iranian election protesters to use the service to share information about results in real-time, reflecting the service's importance as an information-sharing tool.

And it's not just about gaining access to data on current events, but also access to daily, personalized events where social networks can help kids learn about everyday topics and how high-tech citizens interact. What's more, the global reach of social networks allows kids to easily make relationships with friends from all over the world, even though they may have only met face-to-face once, or sometimes never at all, exposing them to a broader range of international influences than ever before. Sites like Facebook also teach a form of heightened empathy for others, as outpourings of positive sentiments are common whenever a friend posts a distressing status update or request for well-wishes. With all the happy news (birthday reminders, engagements, news of new births, etc.) spread on these services as well, social networks can ultimately teach kids about ways to positively interact with others to strengthen social bonds.

Forming Powerful Communities – Many kids have unique interests, and while they may struggle to find others with similar interests in their schools, chances are they can find a thriving and passionate base of like-minded individuals via social networks. These connections help prevent children, including those at risk or faced with physical or psychological challenges, from feeling isolated.

Dr. Paula Tallal, professor of neuroscience at Rutgers University, says that "social media is training us for the environment we live in now," noting that it's a great tool for building communities where none existed before. Tallal gives the example of kids texting or tweeting about a class or lecture, and then forming study groups based on these interactions.

Social media sites are even expanding from general interest topics to more specific uses that benefit society. For example, sites have been created for medical purposes such as dealing with life-altering diseases, alcoholism, drug addiction, weight loss, and autism. Social networking sites with a specific focus help introduce people to others who are dealing with similar issues and provide information, contacts, peer support, and encouragement.

Some mental health professionals have actually found social media platforms to be an especially useful tool for "peer support," where kids and tweens can get guidance and support from professionals and other concerned parties simply by being connected to them. In a recent interview, Temple University psychologist Mark Salzer notes that for a significant number of folks, social media can be "quite meaningful." Even if a bad or negative comment is occasionally observed, he says, there are usually others who chime in with the correct message. Incredibly, studies have shown that literally hundreds of millions of people have received positive support during major life events ranging from job transitions to the loss of a family member from social networks.

SUMMARY

There's a reason why people use social networks by the billions, and it's because they are useful tools that can provide a boundless number of positive benefits. The good news: Parents can rest easy knowing that the vast majority of users are just as careful and thoughtful as you and your kids. But what about those who aren't? Now that you're ready to get your kids connected online via social networks, in the following section, we'll take a closer look at the issues and individuals you need to watch out for to ensure that your family can enjoy a positive online experience.

DANGERS AND CONCERNS

Although we've outlined many ways that kids can benefit from social networks, it would be foolish to pretend that there aren't potential dangers surrounding them as well. Similarly, while most kids use these services with nothing but good intentions, there are certain aspects of the social networking experience that families should be cautious of. Case in point: Social networks are among the most public of spaces, and one in which information and thoughts have the power to travel further, faster than ever before – tremendous care must be taken with what information we choose to post and share.

But let's not get ahead of ourselves. The first thing to note when assessing the possible pitfalls of social networks is as follows: Like millions of others who safely and responsibly utilize these services every day, odds are, your child will enjoy a positive experience upon them. However, whenever kids take part in any sort of high-tech activity with associated risks, parents must also make a point of proactively assessing these concerns and possible worst-case scenarios. This not only includes considering the actual likelihood that something bad will happen, but – as precautionary measure – planning solutions that you can employ if it does. Not only is forewarned forearmed, but the more you educate yourself and your children about these concerns, the better

equipped you and your family will be to deal with them should they arise.

In the case of social networks and other online activities, it bears considering. As with other forms of technology and media, mainstream press tends to fixate on headline-grabbing examples of select incidents which occur on these platforms, rather than routine exchanges and day–to–day interactions, and equate negative behaviors with extreme consequences, when in fact mistakes are made every day which do not lead to severe consequences. (Kids will be kids, and forced to learn lessons, in every aspect of life – not just virtual.) Rather than view all social networks with fear or trepidation, it's best to consider them a neutral tool, or platform for connectivity, as with any other piece of hardware, software or technology – how we and others choose to use them defines what we take away from the experience. Despite what you may see on TV, not every choice made on social networks is a matter of life and death. However, many related worries are also perfectly valid and should not be taken lightly – there are indeed pressing dangers and concerns that every family should be aware of here, which can range from periodic annoyances and nuisances to exchanges and interactions that may prompt serious legal and financial repercussions.

Popular resource ConnectSafely.org identifies the following risk factors to look for amongst kids using social networks to help parents gauge concerns when considering how likely it is that their children will encounter negative behavior online:

• Those who act aggressively online are more than twice as likely to be victimized online, so make sure to keep an eye on how your children behave on social media sites. If they're prone to react angrily or impulsively in real life, and make heated remarks in the spur of the moment that they may regret later, they're likely to duplicate that behavior online to the potential detriment of themselves or others.

• The most common risk for young people on social networks surrounds negative content or interactions that have been shared or initiated by their peers, whether you're looking at harassment, offensive remarks, age-inappropriate material or aggressive or hurtful behavior. Be cognizant of whom your child is interacting with, what material they're consuming, and the types of exchanges that occur within such services' confines.

• Not all children are equally at-risk online. Note that if a child's offline personality or real-life history involves incidents where they've been prone to suffering harassment or experiencing negative behavior at the hand of others, they're also more likely to encounter similar issues online.

Many other issues – challenges at home, trouble interacting with peers, poor communications or social skills, behavioral issues, a poor grasp of privacy concerns or lack of empathy for others, etc. – may make children susceptible to risk as well. You are advised to take all into account when considering the potential for trouble on these services. Bearing in mind that the vast majority of children will eventually find their way onto social networks, however, attempting to shield them alone is seldom enough to address potential concerns. Knowing that the day may well come when children make the leap onto social networks, despite your desire to keep these tools away from them, we must also educate both ourselves and our kids about these platforms, and how to properly and safely utilize them.

It may bring comfort to remember, though: Many socially-awkward or at-risk children mature and grow into perfectly healthy and well-balanced adults – so too can they come to be responsible digital citizens. Take the time to invest in your family's future by preparing kids for life in the virtual world, noting that social networks will only become an increasing part of its normal course going forward: It's a decision that will pay dividends for all involved. That said, even having made a commitment to ongoing education and fostering positive, open dialogue in the household surrounding these topics, we nonetheless need to ask ourselves an important question, given that troubles can and often do arise: What is it about social networks that make it so easy for kids to make mistakes online?

Blame the degree of anonymity that social network users appear to enjoy, which can easily lead to the oversharing of information. Comfortably seated in our homes before the mirror of inanimate computer monitors, laptops and smartphones, it's easy to forget that these devices actually serve as both a window and gateway to project ourselves onto an ever-changing world where words and thoughts can touch millions, and live on forever in perpetuity. Even well-known celebrities, politicians and sports figures have made epic mistakes, tweeting offensive jokes, posting inappropriate photos and even slandering other people or ethnic groups, because they forget to behave themselves, and that the entire world is watching. Consider actor Ashton Kutcher's ill-informed support of controversial figures involved in a high-profile court case or the career-ending salacious photos that politician Anthony Weiner tweeted publicly, both of which led to severe consequences.

Similarly, it's all too easy to convince ourselves that we're safe and secure within online confines, as social networks' personal nature creates the illusion of intimacy, when in fact they're as public a space as any town square or subway platform – perhaps more so, as millions may be present. The very definition of friend – in the past, someone we knew and enjoyed spending time with in real-life – has changed in the modern dictionary as a result of the growth of social networks, which instead assign the title to any online connection. Many kids have 'friends' on Facebook that they've never met in real life, and Twitter, Reddit and Pinterest are rife with friend lists that contain complete strangers. So ask yourself: Why are we and our children comfortable sharing so much with people we may have encountered only in brief passing, if ever, in our day-to-day lives? Again, appearances can be deceiving. Here, it pays to be paranoid, but not overly so: While most people won't misuse information gained thereby, it only takes one bad apple to painfully take advantage of intimate, personal and private details shared on social networks to our detriment. Therefore it's crucial to be safe, smart and responsible in how we use them – an ounce of prevention far outweighs a pound of cure.

HINTS, TIPS AND ADVICE FOR USING SOCIAL NETWORKS

As noted, a little bit of safety and common sense can go a long way towards keeping both yourself and your kids out of trouble and danger when usingany social network. Before digging deeper into specific issues and concerns, and how to address these topics, let's pause to consider a few basic guidelines for responsible usage, which can help you and your kids avoid many common mistakes.

• Parents and educators should explain to children that everything done, said, or shared on the Internet needs to be treated as if it's public, visible to sensitive parties, and cannot be taken back. Because it can't: Once a statement is made, it's out there potentially for the entire world – including significant others, college recruiters, parents, teachers, and future employees – to see, and even if you remove the post from your profile or timeline, it's likely to have already been seen by others, and in some cases may have been re–shared with third parties. Always think twice before hitting the post or share button, especially if you find yourself in a highly emotional state.

• Don't share any photos or other information that may paint yourself or others in an embarrassing, unflattering or controversial light. If a subject raises even the slightest question in your mind, it's best to just erase it before hitting the "post," "tweet," or "share" button.

• Don't spread rumors, innuendo, name–calling and negative gossip. Or, in other words, if you don't have something nice to say, don't say it – negativity never reflects well on the individual spreading it. Likewise, if you're not willing to say something directly to another's face in real life, then don't do so publicly for the world to see.

• Don't be afraid to ask others to remove photos, videos, comments, posts or items in which you're tagged from their social network profile which you don't approve of. Friends won't want to do anything which could offend you or make you feel uncomfortable, and the request will likely even spark dialogue as to what is and isn't appropriate to be sharing.

• Don't announce where you are, where you are going or where you will be, especially as it pertains to family vacations or other instances when you may be away from your home for lengthy periods. Revealing location information makes it easy for others to pinpoint when family members are away, children may be vulnerable, and/or when your house will be completely empty – e.g. a prime target for a robbery.

• Reserve the right to delete unwanted postings or comments from your profile that others have made, but also make sure you and your kids are doing so for the right reasons. Posts that respectfully disagree or argue a point are part of a healthy online dialogue – it's important to acknowledge others' opinions and viewpoints. However, updates that cross the line can and should be removed: Let logic and good judgment be your guides here.

• Do not accept friend requests from strangers on social networking sites, and configure your profile so that information and media is only being shared with approved contacts. Among the most basic privacy protection steps, these are also among the most powerful – providing unknown users access to posts and photos potentially exposes you to danger.

• Get up-to-speed on all the privacy settings that are available on the social networks that you use. On Facebook in particular, privacy settings frequently change, so it's important to check them regularly and ensure that your information is protected. We delve into more details on online privacy below.

It's imperative that you and your children are both consistently looking for and can identify behaviors and patterns that increase their risks for encountering online dangers on social networks, and know how to properly react if such issues are ever encountered. As part of this education, let's begin by taking a closer look at the most common dangers and concerns kids may face when it comes to social networks. Afterwards, we'll look at a number of trends surrounding these influencers, and how they're evolving over time. Again – staying up to date and informed with new developments, trends

and updates in both kids' online lives and social network services themselves is a powerful first line of defense in the battle to keep children safe online.

ONLINE PRIVACY

Among the biggest concerns for any user on social networks today – parents and kids included – is online privacy. According to Norton Online Safety expert Marian Merritt, more parents are actually concerned that their kids will give out too much personal information online than are concerned about their kids interacting with dangerous people or being exposed to indecent information. Although many experts are critical of the way the company has chosen to do so, it's worth nothing that Facebook has in fact taken many steps to give users at least some semblance of control over the information that they are sharing, even though access to such information can be extremely valuable to such a company and the marketers whose dollars help support it. Google has also taken steps to update and unify its privacy policies across all the company's platforms, including Google+ and YouTube, allowing users to easily configure and control personal settings across all Google properties.

Obviously, the first and most effective step one can take to keep sensitive or personal information private is not to share it in the first place. But on a social network, where people go to specifically connect and communicate with other individuals, there's a certain implicit "quid pro quo" expectation that everyone who's connected will participate in some sort of exchange of information, and do so in a way that's more personal than professional. Luckily, there are steps that you can take to keep posts and media that you share, from status updates to photos to location check-ins, as private as you'd like these details to remain while still enjoying the basic benefits and fun of social networks.

Many of these tweaks, which you can make to your profile once logged in, are pretty straightforward. Alas, many others are found in unexpected places, or layered deep within settings section sub-menus that can make such features difficult to find unless you know exactly what you're looking for. Note that this is a common criticism of social networks: That while many make it possible to control privacy specific settings, they don't always make the process of doing so simple, straightforward and easy. But it is worth considering that such options are available, and a simple online search query or scan of social network sites' help sections is often enough to help you sniff them out with a little research.

Here are several of the most common privacy concerns kids and their parents need to be aware of when it comes to safeguarding their information on social networks.

WHO CAN SEE WHAT YOU POST

You may not realize it, but you can control who can see your status updates, photos, check-ins, videos and other information that you post. This is a key feature of Google+, but a lesser-known feature on sites like Facebook. Many sites offer options within every post to allow you to select who can enjoy access to them, and within most networks' privacy settings menu, you can configure your default settings for different types of updates so that they may automatically only be seen by friends, the public or yourself alone. Among the most basic forms of privacy controls, it's one which many users are increasingly becoming attuned to.

WHO CAN CONNECT TO YOU

Did you know that you can control settings regarding whether or not you can be found with a casual search, who is allowed to send you friend requests, and who can send you messages? Many social networks allow users to decide if they wish to be publicly searchable, if anyone can connect with them, or they'd prefer to limit requests and interactions to personal acquaintances, or friends of existing friends. In the case of receiving messages, many also allow you to limit connectivity so only pre-approved friends can pass notes along.

POSTING AND TAGGING

A big plus with several social networks is that you can also control which forms of information others can post on your profile. The first basic choice to make is whether or not you will allow others to post on your wall. Typically, unless you're a public figure and/or especially sensitive to topics being discussed, it's fine to let others post on your wall, as the friends in your network are unlikely to post something inappropriate. But if you're nervous about the possibility, you can simply choose to prohibit others from posting on your wall, and the only time they're likely to complain about it is on your birthday or other special occasions.

Many networks' privacy settings also offer another layer of protection against other users posting things to their profile that they can't control, e.g. tagging them in status updates or sharing photos or videos that may paint them in an unflattering light. If you still want to allow this activity, but maintain some level of influence over it, some networks provide the option to let none of your friends see the information others post (i.e. limit it so that it's visible only to you). Alternately, you can limit visibility to friends, or those who are connected to your current friends. You can also do the same for check-ins you're tagged in. Many social network sites also use facial recognition software to detect users' presence in photos, and you can control whether or not to allow these features to suggest

tagging images with your profile to friends when they upload photos of you. You can also choose to approve or remove any tags users have created.

GEO-LOCATION SERVICES AND CHECK-INS

One increasingly popular element of many social networks is the ability to check in at specific places on the map to let others know where you are, e.g. signing in to a local bar or restaurant and sharing this location with friends online. While it can be fun to check in and hear stories from others that either are there as well or have been to the place before, the fact is that doing so reveals to everyone that follows to exactly where you are at present, and where you aren't – both of which can be dangerous pieces of information in the wrong hands.

Happily, it's easy to avoid traps here – simply elect not to check-in. But you'll also want to disable location-based services from your profile's settings menu, and on any Internet-connected devices (ex: laptop, smartphone or tablet) so as not to inadvertently include this information in posts. The FBI also recently warned families against another danger of posting images online: The use of geolocation tags embedded in photos that can be publicly accessed, thereby revealing exactly where on earth the picture was taken. This could be dangerous because, when performing even an action as innocent as sharing family photos, you could be unwittingly letting others know where you live and work. Check your camera and/or smartphone's manual for information on how to disable the location tagging of photos, and we also recommend disabling any and all features associated with "Location Services" on your social network accounts.

THIRD PARTY ACCESS TO INFORMATION

Third parties' ability to access your personal and/or private information sits at the crux of many of today's biggest social network privacy debates. While COPPA provides an additional layer of protection for kids under the age of 13, concerns surround just how much information these networks themselves are sharing directly with external parties (e.g. marketing companies or advertisers), and how much data is being shared with the makers of popular apps by virtue of their usage. In a way, social networks are faced with a puzzling proposition, because users want an experience that is simple, intuitive and – most importantly – seemingly personally tailored, which requires at least some basic knowledge of users' details and routine habits. But this information – which can be extremely valuable for those seeking insights about specific users or demographics – is highly powerful: Users also don't want anyone

to misuse, mistreat or mishandle their personal data.

As an example, according to the Facebook's Privacy Settings page, "your name, profile picture, gender, networks, username, and user ID are always publicly available, including to Apps." The reason for this, the company says, is to make this information more social. Naysayers argue that the reasons are more financially driven in nature – many companies or unscrupulous individuals would pay a premium to get access to said data. Wherever you sit on the issue, it's crucial to consider: Any information you share on social networks can and may be accessible to others, and should be doled out judiciously as a result. You'll also want to read the fine print in any social network or app's Terms of Service carefully – even the act of signing up for service or filling out your profile may cause you to grant permission social networks or apps to access and redistribute this information.

On the bright side, modern social networks often provide users a level of control over which information is shared, and to what extent, with third parties, which is extremely important because such providers are separate entities that have different privacy and operating policies than the social network itself. Moreover, many apps can gain access to information on users' friends, so even those who don't actively register to use the app may find their data inadvertently exposed for others' viewing. It's important that you not only regulate which information can be shared on social networks, such as your age, location, birthday, photos, status updates or other material. You must also be cognizant of who has access to it, and how. Settings menus do provide some level of control over others' access to information: At a bare minimum, you should familiarize yourself with and take advantage of these options.

ACCESS TO YOUR PAST HISTORY

What we post on our profiles is recorded, often in perpetuity, and archives may be available for viewing dating several years back, e.g. to your wayward teen years, when you were less old and wise. If you're concerned about previous activity being seen, note that some social networks allow you to easily change privacy settings on all previous posts, so you can retroactively limit access. If a change of heart or life event has made you suddenly become more private in nature, or concerned about who has access to information, the option to lock down previous information may be available. However, not all services offer this feature – it's something to consider before registering for service on select networks, or posting updates that may later come back to haunt you.

Recently, Facebook has made it possible to go back and change the settings on

your past history to be the same, but if you want to control every single update you've ever done individually, it's a time-intensive process that requires going through and changing settings on each one. But a good first step is to make your profile or Timeline private, which will prevent the general public from viewing your posts.

BLOCKING ACCESS BY UNWANTED USERS

If someone is harassing you, or you'd prefer not to be connected to specific individuals for a variety of reasons, you can add them to a "Block" list (or similarly delineated blacklist feature) which prevents them from issuing friend requests or sending you app and event invites. You can also choose to block specific apps from accessing your profile and interacting with you.

On Facebook, where both friends must opt-in to be connected, either user may terminate the relationship at any time by defriending, and you will no longer be connected until both agree again. As with many things on Facebook, the status of sent friend requests as well as defriending is handled rather discreetly, with no real notifications that actions have or haven't been taken.

For Twitter, Pinterest and other services where following is only a one-way decision, the option to block users can come in handy should you come across spammers or other contacts who are engaging in inappropriate ways. Noting this though, it's not particularly common for folks who know each other to need to block one another on a routine basis. Rather, it's usually a safeguard against the worst the Internet has to offer.

SUMMARY

Cheerfully, for all these concerns, a recent TRUSTe survey of both parents and teens investigating their privacy habits and preferences on social networks found that, for the most part, "the kids are alright," noting that a majority of teens use privacy controls on social networks and that most parents actively monitor their teen's privacy. But there's still room for improvement here, with more than 2/3 of teens confessing that they'd accepted a Facebook friend request from someone they didn't know, and nearly one in ten teens admitting to accepting all friend requests they receive.

In 2012, an FTC proposal was also enacted that was designed to close loopholes in the 1998 Children's Online Privacy Protection Act, (COPPA). When COPPA was introduced in the late '90s, it set the standard for sites around the globe to maintain safeguards and privacy settings designed to protect against marketing to and the collection of information from any users under the age of 13. However, the simple fact that the original act was created in 1998 in a world before Facebook, Twitter and even Google meant that it was in desperate need of a fresh look. The FTC itself acknowledged that COPPA was in need of updating in its revised proposals, but stated that it remained committed to "helping to create a safer, more secure online experience for children" even with the "rapid-fire pace of technological change" providing a challenge with regard to meeting the originally stated COPPA goals.

These COPPA changes are important to parents both for what they do and they do not cover. Before the updates, many sites were able to claim they weren't responsible for adhering to these more stringent standards even though they were clearly aimed at kids, because the site also targeted older users. But, as a US law, COPPA also can't govern sites that are operated out of foreign countries, even though many will voluntarily comply with the standards. So parents need to know that just because COPPA helps hold companies and sites to a high standard when it comes to dealing with kids and information, it doesn't mean that everyone adheres to it.

So why is the issue of marketing to kids so important – important enough for the FTC be involved? Because DVRs and the ability to pre-record programs, watch them at any time, and skip commercials, coupled with the rise of connected solutions like smartphones and tablets, have changed the way in which children both watch TV and consume information, and therefore greatly impacted the way in which advertisers can reach youthful audiences – much marketing outreach now occurs online. And despite restrictions adopted by social networking sites to restrict usage of these platforms by children under 13 years of age, a recent survey from research firm SodaHead revealed that more than half of parents with 12 year-olds allowed them to utilize Facebook, nearly a third of 11 year-olds already had an account on the service, and one in five 10 year-olds were already using the site in violation of its terms of service – thereby potentially exposing children's private data to advertisers.

Marketers naturally want to reach young demographics, and sway them towards buying new products: The tween audience alone, according to research firm EPM Communications, is responsible for $43 billion in annual spending. Because of this, it's up to us as parents and caregivers to be wary of the information that children share and consume, so that personal data isn't just kept safe and secure, but also so that children can make informed, unbiased decisions. Granted, there's no vast evil conspiracy out there secretly scheming to steal your child's private data and use it to relentlessly market to, influence, and sell them new goods or services. But the more individuals who have access to your child's information, the more potential points of risk presented,

through opportunities for both data breach and contact by unwanted parties. Among the most vulnerable and inexperienced of netizens, it's important that we help educate and inform children about such issues, and take all necessary steps and precautions to protect their privacy.

CYBERBULLYING

Cyberbullying is another issue that concerns many parents and educators about kids' use of social networks. Cyberbullying occurs whenever someone uses a social network or other form of electronic communication to harm or demean others in a deliberate or hostile matter. Instances could range from something seemingly innocent, like the sharing of an unflattering picture, to something more serious, like a threat with malicious intent.

Case in point: Recently, a father in Minnesota captured the cyberbullying of his adopted African American daughter by videotaping threats made online. What's interesting to note is this father not only captured the evidence, but he fought back using social media, by posting his concerns onto YouTube. As a result, not only did he stop the incidence of bullying, but the bully's father was fired from his job.

Granted, concerns over kids and bullying certainly aren't new: The schoolyard bully has been a staple in children's literature, movies and real–life anecdotes for centuries. But what makes bullying so much more prevalent these days is the many more methods that those with malicious intent can utilize in order to torment their victims, and to a much broader extent. The media has focused on cyberbullying as a key concern for anyone using the Internet today, especially kids. Thankfully, the public is being provided growing exposure to knowledge surrounding the epidemic, and schools, parents and educators are increasingly working together to provide anti–bullying curriculums to children starting at a very young age.

Unfortunately, the impetus for this heightened awareness in many cases is a result of tragic tales of kids who've suffered at the hands of bullies. In recent years, the aforementioned story of Tyler Clementi, as well as others such as Jamey Rodemeyer and Megan Meier, all ended in suicide after negative online experiences. Meier was a teenager who was baited into a fake online relationship by a jealous friend's mother. And Rodemeyer endured negative comments from others about his sexual orientation, including a few who expressed that they didn't care whether he was dead or alive. Needless to say, comments made or negative actions we're exposed to online can cut every bit as deep as those encountered in the real world – and oftentimes can cross the boundaries which separate each.

But while there's no doubt that social media and high-tech tools played a role in these individuals' tragic tales, experts agree that these are extreme examples – not the norm. Nevertheless, they underscore the grave and potentially fatal consequences that words and actions encountered on social networks can have on the lives of others. Therefore it's imperative that we treat others with the same dignity, respect and kindness that we do in our real lives, and with the same level of consideration that we ask for ourselves.

Because of the broad range of acts that can be considered cyberbullying, estimates on its scope and frequency vary. However, according to various sources, between one third and one half of all kids online have been subjected to some form of online harassment. Major social networks like Facebook, Google+, Twitter and more have therefore taken strong stands against cyberbullying, and incorporate policies into their terms of use which specifically prohibit the practice. Violations can lead to users being blocked, banned or removed. But censors cannot be everywhere all the time – unfortunately, the sad truth is that much of the responsibility for dealing with these incidences falls to families and victims themselves.

As parents, you must make sure that your children know that online harassment is never okay, whether they themselves are the victims or they are merely witnesses to negative online behavior. Whether reading a disparaging joke or unseemly comment about others, or observing more negative behavior as it happens online, kids need to be cognizant of what to do when they see or think they may be privy to or involved in a cyberbullying incident. For starters, they need to be aware that the first step is to alert you or another trusted adult. It's also a good idea to keep a log of all such incidents so that you have a written record of the behavior. To this extent, we recommend learning how to take a screenshot on your computer or mobile device to capture the info, as the bully may eventually attempt to delete the material. Likewise, if your child is being cyberbullied, make sure that they do not respond, as doing so only provides added incentive for bullies to continue engaging in negative behavior. Serious incidences should further be reported to qualified experts or law enforcement authorities. In all cases, children should be made aware from the moment that they set foot on social networks that unconditional help and support is available — and where to turn should they require it.

When you are having conversations with your kids about cyberbullying, make sure to focus on the positive. Researchers have pointed out that teenagers' cultural frames of reference leave them ill-equipped to feel like a victim or as if they're oppressed. Teenagers feel empowered, strong (and sometimes invincible, which as we know is what leads to many typical teenage problems). Encourage empathy and focus on positive concepts like healthy relationships and digital citizenship rather than the negatively charged concept of bullying.

TIPS FOR PARENTS

• Teach kids to treat all individuals encountered online with fairness and respect. The same courtesies you extend to others at school or on the playground should be extended to the virtual realm as well.

• Adults must proactively educate and equip kids to make safe, responsible online decisions. Teaching positive behaviors and healthy computing habits starting at the earliest age is essential.

• Parents should create an open, honest household dialogue with children and encourage them to come forward with questions or concerns should they encounter strange, uncomfortable or disturbing online interactions.

CYBERSTALKING AND HARASSMENT

Cyberstalking is an even more personal form of cyberbullying, and involves the constant and repetitive use of e-mails, messages, videos or other online communication to contact or interact with a recipient who does not wish to receive them. Cyberharassment is slightly different than cyberstalking in that it is generally defined as not involving a credible threat. For example, cyberharassment may consist of a user simply sending threatening or harassing communications on social networks, but with no real intent to follow through in real life on their actions.

According to the National Conference of State Legislatures, most states have enacted anti-cyberstalking or anti-cyberharassment laws, or have laws that explicitly include electronic forms of communication within overarching laws prohibiting more traditional forms of stalking or harassment. In addition, recent concerns about protecting minors from online bullying or harassment have led to an increase in states' enactment of specific laws prohibiting high-tech methods of harassment, as discussed above.

Be certain that you and your kids know how to use the built-in controls on social networks to help report any negative behavior encountered, as well as block any users engaging in harassment from contacting you or your children again. Also be certain you and your children know where to turn for help should these methods prove inadequate to deter ongoing harassment, and know where support and professional assistance can be found as well.

IDENTITY THEFT AND ID PROTECTION

According to the most recent data available from the FTC, less than 1% of identity theft victims were under 19 years old. But let's not celebrate by posting our kids' birthdays, best friend's names or information about the schools that they attend online for the world to see just yet. Case in point: Many experts think these statistics are inaccurate, and underreport the problem, as many families don't discover identity theft until their children are around the age of 18 and beginning to enter the workforce or college and attempt to access their own credit reports for the first time. In fact, a survey from ID Analytics estimated that 140,000 incidents of identity fraud are perpetrated against minors each year. And FTC identity protection specialist Steve Toporoff recently told an NBC investigator that "recent studies suggest child identity theft is more prevalent than even identity theft against adults."

To help protect your family, make sure your kids understand what constitutes private information. An easy way to do this is to let them know that anything that can be used to identify them in real life should be considered off-limits for public sharing. More than likely, they're going to be letting the world see their given name if they use a social network like Facebook or Google+. However, other identifying information, such phone numbers, addresses, schools or even favorite places to hang out should be protected and only shared when absolutely necessary and with a grown-up's permission.

Each family will have their own rules for what's appropriate for posting online, and what information they're comfortable sharing with the public in general. And while your own household may be comfortable sharing information about every family member's latest life happenings or the newest news at work, others may be much more sensitive – so, when engaging in online exchanges, it's also important you respect others and default to acting as if they want nothing personal shared about themselves, so as not to impinge on their privacy. After all, just as you want your kids to control the information that they're sharing, so too will others wish for your children to treat their own personal info with similar respect.

As an aside, identity protection services like may be worth considering for your family if identity theft is an issue that you are particularly concerned about. For as little as $10 a month, these and other services promise to monitor credit reports and other sensitive data to detect and guard against potential incidences of fraud in the making. Once a year, you can also check up on your whole family's credit reports free by visiting:

www.annualcreditreport.com.

DEVELOPMENTAL CONCERNS

Amongst many parents and grandparents who are not familiar with social networks, a common complaint is that social networks are full of too much pointless or wasteful information, and promote amongst children both increasing narcissism and shorter attention spans. To this end, in a recent appearance before the UK's House of Lords to discuss the impact of social networks on developing brains, top neuroscientist Baroness Susan Greenfield from Oxford University warns of what she calls the lifelong effects of too much social networking.

According to Greenfield, social networks "are infantilizing [our brains] into the state of [that possessed by] small children who are attracted by buzzing noises and bright lights, who have a short attention span and live for the moment." As she puts it, "If the young brain is exposed from the outset to a world of fast action and reaction, of instant new screen images flashing up with the press of a key, such rapid interchange might accustom the brain to operate over such timescales." In other words, she claims, social media promotes juvenile behavior and instant gratification – strong sentiments, indeed. Social networks, Greenfield claims, produce "a much more marked preference for the here-and-now, where the immediacy of an experience trumps any regard for the consequences."

These sites can provide a "constant reassurance" as well as a distancing from the "stress" of real-life, face-to-face conversations, the most prized form of interpersonal communications.

Some teachers have likewise expressed concerns that the wide acceptance of sloppy spelling and misuse of grammar among all forms of high communications popular with teens, including social networks, are having a measurable effect on students' classroom skills. Whether it's because pupils are less willing to follow grammatical rules or simply because they hastily complete homework so they can quickly return to connecting with others, they argue, the media landscape is drastically different for kids than it was even five just years ago.

But it probably won't surprise you to hear that there are doctors arguing the opposite viewpoint, and that in fact many of these claims are a bit extreme. Dr. Susan Kraut Whitborn recently published an article in Psychology Today that argues that social networks can actually improve brain function. By allowing folks to stay in touch with a broad range of people and connecting them in ways beyond real-life meetings, she says that using Facebook might even give a part of your brain called the amygdala a boost, which could also be especially beneficial to senior citizens.

ONLINE PREDATORS

The National Center for Missing and Exploited Children conducted a recent study showing that one in every seven children is apt to be sexually solicited online. Most of these contacts are from peers, rather than strangers, but it's hard to consider this good news, except in the context that fears about the general prevalence of online sexual predators may be overblown.

Similarly, while some social networks provide built-in safeguards against connecting with strangers, others easily allow unknown parties to contact and send unsolicited messages to users. (Although such options can typically be turned off by utilizing privacy settings and parental controls). In all cases, the overwhelming odds are that most individuals children will encounter online are perfectly normal, well-adjusted adults. However, to prevent such instances from occurring, and protect children from harm, it's imperative that we educate both kids and ourselves about the related dangers.

To begin with, be certain that your kids understand basic rules of social networkingthat can help prevent them from exchanges with sexual predators. For starters, contact and interactions with strangers should be curtailed as much as possible on these services. While settings should be configured to prevent contact by unknown parties, kids should likewise be taught never to start or engage in conversations with people they don't know. Certainly, reasonable exceptions exist, such as participating in a chat about a favorite TV show or movie on its Facebook fan page, or participating in public threads about innocuous everyday discussion topics such as different types of music or the latest headline news. However, parents should be aware of the arenas in which any such discussions are occurring, who is involved in any such dialogue, and – in all cases – private exchanges with strangers should be tightly regulated or prohibited outright.

While it may seem obvious, it likewise bears reminding your kids that they shouldn't be sending out personal photos online to unknown individuals, and should never arrange a face-to-face meeting with someone they met online without adult permission and supervision. Kids should also be taught to recognize the danger signs that may indicate the presence of an online predator, and to immediately contact a parent or trusted adult if they think someone is soliciting them online. Definitions of 'suspicious' behavior differ amongst individuals and households, and it's imperative to let logic be your guide here when weighing the scenario. However, as a general rule, if any action makes you or your children feel suspicious or uncomfortable, it's best to err on the side of caution, and remember

that online, everyone is, to some extent, playing a character.

SEXTING

Sexting – the practice of sending sexually explicit text or multimedia messages – first became part of the widespread public vernacular as part of a 2008 survey from CosmoGirl and the National Campaign to Prevent Teen and Unplanned Pregnancy. When the duo unveiled some shocking numbers about the nature and frequency of related images being shared, it opened many parents' and researchers' eyes to the magnitude and extent that teens may be transmitting sexually-explicit come-ons or images to one another.

According to the controversial survey, 20% of teens overall and 11% of young teen girls between 13 and 16 reported that they had sent or posted nude or semi-nude pictures or video of themselves via connected sharing methods. And 39% of teens reported sending or posting sexually suggestive messages, with 48% saying they have received such messages – more than enough to make a parent blush.

Nonetheless, it may reassure families to note that many dissenting experts assert that these results are inaccurate and sensationalized due to the self-reporting methodology of the study, with more accurate numbers being that only 1% of teens have appeared in sexually explicit pictures, and only 7% have received photos. A 2012 study from the American Academy of Pediatrics Journal found similar results, indicating that a mere 10% of youths who use the Internet reported appearing in, creating or receiving sexually suggestive images – still, however, more than enough to raise eyebrows amongst any concerned caregivers.

As indicated above, sexting involves the transmission or receipt of sexually explicit material to or from other contacts, and while the practice implies communication via mobile devices, it can often happen over social networks as well. The important thing for children to understand here isn't just that doing so is wrong – it's that engaging in such activities can and likely will come back to hurt them. Case in point: Once indecent images are shared, they're out there for the entire world to potentially see – even if sent to only one "friend," they can spread like wildfire, and there's no way to control them or put the genie back in the proverbial bottle. Ergo, one bad decision here – possibly visible to family members, college recruiters, significant others, future employers, etc. – can come back to haunt those who make it for the rest of their lives.

With the recent rise of an app called Snapchat, parents have even more cause for concern when it comes to texting and sexting. Snapchat enables anyone to post a photograph to fellow users of the application, and the poster has the option for the photo to automatically delete (in other words, self-destruct) within 1–10 seconds, or whatever timeframe the person designates. The app has truly taken off in the teen/early 20s demographic and of course, sexting pictures and lewd images may comprise a sizable portion of the material being shared. The relative anonymity of the app, coupled with the almost immediate disintegration of the image, is what's giving kids the guts to put themselves and their bodies out there. But of course, as with any app or social network, there are loopholes and people have figured out how to take screenshots of these images, no longer keeping them as fleeting (and disappearing) snapshots. There's no doubt that other kinds of technology like this will continue to appear and inundate children, and it's up to parents to figure out how to best regulate their privacy and keep lines of communication open. However content may be shared, no matter how strict one's privacy settings, kids need to learn to assume that nothing they post to a social network or online should be considered private, even if it would appear to be that way at the outset. Once you've shared content, be it in the form of a photo, video or status update, it's safe to assume you've lost control of the information, which anyone may and can gain access to and co-opt. Before hitting "Send," "Post" or "Tweet" on any update, a good rule of thumb is to consider whether you'd be comfortable with your grandmother seeing the update in question. If not, you may want to think twice about what you're about to transmit, given that it has the potential to reach even the most unintended audiences, and live on in perpetuity forever.

Parents need to make sure that the topic of sexting and the sharing of sexual images is part of any honest and frank sexual discussion that they're having with their kids. Just as children must learn to keep certain parts of their bodies and activities private, they must also learn to protect images of their body as well – and not expose them in the most public of forums. Children need to consider how messages may be received as well. Imagine a girl who thinks she's just being silly or joking by sending a sexually-charged picture – who's to say the boy who sees it won't take it as a sign that she's interested in them?

There's a fascinating offshoot of this issue, too, as it pertains the legal ramifications of sexting. It turns out, the issue's even more complicated because of the severity of child pornography laws. Rather than see teenagers who made a dumb decision out of ineptitude, not malice, charged with crimes that could ruin their lives and/or permanent records, some commentators have actually recommended that parents don't get authorities involved if they discover sexting because of the potential long-lasting negative legal ramifications. Consider that since minors are involved, crimes like "the transmission of pornographic images of children" can have lifelong negative repercussions, or even lead to potential jail time. However, the National Center for Missing and Exploited Youth reports only one case in which a sexter was treated as a sex offender, and dealt with accordingly harshly. For safety's sake, it's best to loop in authorities, school administrators and local law enforcement officials, especially if there are instances of harassment involved – this is a serious issue that demands the involvement of qualified professionals. But it's surprising to hear some experts recommend against that.

SPAM AND CLICKJACKING

Spam (unwanted or promotional messages sent by unsolicited parties) is a huge problem for anyone that uses e-mail, and one that has now invaded social networks. Whether you're seeing sponsored or fraudulent stories appear in a newsfeed, or being subjected to explicit links or product advertisements on Twitter disguised as shortened links, social network spam is designed to take advantage of these services' sharing and connecting capabilities. Essentially, the sender hopes you'll click on links and/or share them with friends, potentially exposing yourself and others to harmful computer threats or undesired advertisements.

It's easy to see why spammers and scammers love social networks as a way to spread malware and sales links – material has the chance to spread like wildfire, and is often clicked by unsuspecting friends who believe you've willingly shared it with them. Knowing this, the same practices that can be applied to dealing with e-mail spam should also be adapted to spam designed for social networks. Specifically – don't click on or share unsolicited messages or links whose intent, accuracy and final destinations cannot be verified, or download material without first verifying its origin, source and content. So while a headline or link may look especially titillating or intriguing, teach your kids that what they read online may not be true, and everything they click on could potentially produce negative results.

Adults and kids need to practice extra caution here – if you don't know who sent the update or link, what it contains or where it leads, it's best to proceed with caution. As ever, a healthy sense of paranoia pays.

INAPPROPRIATE CONTENT

Definitions of inappropriate content and language vary by household. Among the most public of spaces though, it's inevitable that children will be exposed to material that falls into this category on social networks at some point during their online sojourns.

Services all take precautions to limit access to explicit material, and filters and settings may be available in select cases that are designed to weed out language or material that's commonly-recognized as inappropriate. But parents need to be aware of how children are interacting, when, whom with, and what exchanges are occurring – automatic controls can only prevent exposure to so much content. Which isn't to say that social networks are a breeding ground for profanity or lewdness (many, in fact, offer a wealth of safe forums in which to play, or are specifically designed to provide age-appropriate contexts), merely that you need to take advantage of all the tools each provides, and teach children about how to respond appropriately when questionable material is (almost inevitably) encountered, with social norms varying by household, country and background.

Should you or your children encounter inappropriate content or exchanges on a social network, don't just report it to site administrators, all of whom have a vested interest in keeping things clean and on the up and up, like any respectable business. Also make sure you and your family know how to ignore, block and steer clear of it, and have both established clear guidelines for what constitutes unacceptable material and rules for addressing and responding to it when encountered up-front.

PSYCHOLOGICAL DISORDERS

The American Academy of Pediatrics recently released a report on the effects of social media on children and adolescents, looking into the issue of whether Facebook use could lead to depression. Many pediatricians reported that after spending time online and on social networks, many teens become angry, irritable or moody.

However, on the heels of this study, a pair of researchers from the University of Wisconsin also found that while the many hours kids spend on social networks account for more than half their time online, there appear to be no distinct associations between time spent social networking and instances of heightened depression."Counseling patients or parents regarding the risk of 'Facebook Depression' may be premature," researchers Lauren A. Jelenchick, Megan A. Moreno and Jens C. Eickhoff explain in the study, published in the Journal of Adolescent Health.

"[Nonetheless,] while the amount of time on Facebook is not associated with depression, we encourage parents to be active role models and teachers on safe and balanced media use for their children," says Moreno. In other words, she says, parents needn't worry about kids' usage of social networks negatively impacting their mood so much as simply making sure it's part of a healthy,

balanced and monitored media diet. The American Academy of Pediatrics actually seconds these findings, saying that teens who experience this so-called "Facebook Depression" usually have a propensity for depression in general. The takeaway here: Although social networks may not necessarily cause depression in your children, it's been posited that these services can amplify these conditions if they are predisposed to them.

Note that in addition to depression, there are other psychological issues such as eating disorders or violence which some critics say social media can also be an amplifier for, with researchers in Germany even coining a term for a new phenomenon called "Facebook Envy." Though the featured sample size was small (about 584 people), they recently published a study entitled, "Envy on Facebook: A Hidden Threat to Users' Life Satisfaction?" that concluded that envy is the biggest negative emotion that people feel after spending time of Facebook, likely from the posts and pictures of extravagant vacations, amazing jobs and perfect children they constantly see on others' profiles.

Research to date remains inconclusive, however. From the standpoint of safety and sensibility, it bears considering – routine exposure to any negative influence can have a lasting and conditioning effect. Happily, many positive influences are found interspersed throughout social networks as well – always consider the topics and individuals being discussed and consumed by your children online.

ADDICTION

Some experts insist that social media can be habit-forming.

According to Dr. Mauricio Delgado, director of the Lab for Social Affective Neuroscience in the Department of Psychology at Rutgers, social media provides a tremendously powerful form ofpositive reinforcement. Just as people respond to encouraging plaudits in real-life, he says, social network users are far more likely to repeat or perform specific behaviors if they are directly followed by something pleasurable, such as receiving a "Like" notice on Facebook or a retweet on Twitter. And these forms of immediate social reinforcement may be tapping directly into the brain's reward circuitry, causing us to become more interested in and dependent on them. Alas, addiction can develop when the pursuit of such rewards becomes compulsive or obsessive, and that's why some believe that many tweens and teens are susceptible to social media addiction.

But Dr. Joan Morrell, a professor of neuroscience at the Rutgers Center for Molecular and Behavioral Neuroscience, noted in a recent news release that in cases where social media has become a severe addiction, the behavior is most likely masking a deeper issue. Social media is "something people turn to," she says, "but it's not the [root of] the problem itself. For those where it has become an addiction, it could be an escape from such underlying issues as depression, anxiety or other mental health disorders." Morrell recommends that if social networking or any other activity you're engaging in isn't allowing you to meet your goals or are interfering with your ability to sleep, eat well and study, you need to reach out for appropriate help.

For now though, the jury remains out, with authorities split in their opinion as to the potentially addictive nature of social networks. Like any other high-tech activity though, communicating through social media is best pursued in moderation and balanced with equal or greater amounts of real-world personal activity and interaction. If you suspect your child is having a problem pulling away from such services, speak to them about your concerns, and, as needed, seek help from qualified professionals.

DEALING WITH MISUSE OF SOCIAL NETWORKS

CyberTipline (www.cybertipline.com) bills itself as the "911 of the Internet" – a place where families can reach out for help and report instances of trouble encountered online. A service of the National Center for Missing & Exploited Youth, administrators urge parents and children to make contact if they see any of the following activities taking place on social networks:

• Possession, Manufacture, and Distribution of Child Pornography
• Online Enticement of Children for Sexual Acts
• Child Prostitution
• Sex Tourism Involving Children
• Extrafamilial Child Sexual Molestation
• Unsolicited Obscene Material Sent to a Child
• Misleading Domain Names
• Misleading Words or Digital Images on the Internet

It's often a good idea to report crimes there as there's often a question of jurisdiction involved since the content may have been posted from one location, hosted on a server found in another locale, and viewed by you from yet another area. CyberTipline can help alert the appropriate officials as to the crime.

In the case of innocent, less serious offenses – e.g. everyday errors made by individuals in their actions online – you might also consider utilizing anysuch infractions as opportunities to teach and inform your children about proper behavior. Health and wellness expert Diane Lang reminds parents that "mistakes are teachable moments that shape our life path." So when your kids

make a simple mistake online, let them know that everyone makes mistakes, and that it's okay to do so – but also use the opportunity to have kids think about what they learned from the exchange and discuss it with you.

Likewise, if something bad happens on social networks or inappropriate behavior occurs and children observe it, explain to your kids what happened and start a dialogue about why the behavior is wrong and ways that such situations can better be handled. For example, if there's an incident of cyberbullying at your school, use it as an opportunity to reinforce correct and appropriate online behaviors, and the importance of treating others with respect and kindness.

DIGITAL CITIZENSHIP

Previously, you've had a chance to learn more about the key features of social networks, what constitutes appropriate behavior upon them, and the potential pitfalls one might face on these services, as well as how to discuss with your children how negative situations might arise on social platforms and how to best address them. But equally important as preparing kids to address possible concerns that may be encountered as a result of virtual interactions with others is making sure that they know how to behave and comport themselves appropriately online.

Think about it like driving. Yes, you want your child to understand the risks associated with riding on the highway, and how to react should they come across belligerent drivers, dangerous weather conditions or the scene of an accident. But just as important as teaching them how to steer around potential pitfalls is how to act responsibly behind the wheel – a concept known as digital citizenship, pioneered by organizations like the Family Online Safety Institute (FOSI). As part of its tenets of safe and respectful online behavior, parents, schools and other high-tech leaders are called upon to embrace the philosophy of preparing students and kids for a connected society by doing their best to teach them about appropriate and positive ways to use and engage with technology.

Mary Beth Hertz, an elementary computer teacher on Edutopia, explains that it's vital that we treat online safety and digital citizenship with the same amount of attention that we give to issues like cyberbullying and online predators. The fact is that kids as young as five and six years of age are joining COPPA-compliant social networks, and also connecting and interacting with children on the Internet in other ways, such as via online video games. To this extent, we must teach all the right way to act from a young age, and how to make good decisions when engaging with Internet-ready devices – not just what to be afraid of or how to respond to incoming threats.

Happily, the concept of digital citizenship encompasses embracing a number of positive behaviors. While we've seen lists that show as many as nine different aspects of the philosophy, here are six core tenets thatappear with recurring frequency, and provide a solid starting foundation for any child:

Education – It's crucial to understand the types of technology and social networks available today, the features such tools support and enable, and how users interact with them – to this extent, it's important that kids, parents and even grandparents are all educated and in full understanding of the many options available.

Etiquette – Proper online etiquette is also crucial for positive high-tech interactions to occur, and governs how kids should behave on social networks and while texting or otherwise communicating with others. We must ask ourselves: What are appropriate ways for kids to use social networks to not only connect with friends and family, but also to assist others, promote the greater good, and give back to your community?

Security – It's important to stay safe online, and a key part of digital citizenship is ensuring the security and sanctity of our information. Whether learning to avoid certain parts of the Internet and social networks, or using programs to help protect ourselves from outside threats, there are active steps you can take to ensure that your data stays safe and secure.

Lifestyle Balance – Yes, technology is an integral part of daily life, but so are real-world encounters, outdoor activities and real-life play. Learning to use technology and social networks in a balanced way can help augment, not subtract from, our real-world interactions.

Respect for Intellectual Property – Understand that real-world laws about creative content and plagiarizing apply online too: Kids must learn to correctly identify and attribute sources when necessary, and why it's not okay to claim material they find on the Internet as their own work.

Sharing and Caring – Since technology plays such an important role in daily life, part of being a digital citizen is working to provide access to technology to all. While the iPad and other tablets have changed learning and what can be done with a seemingly simple app, few do much good to those who can't afford these devices. Digital citizens of all ages are encouraged to be positive contributors to their community, and find ways to extend the benefits of technology to everyone they engage with, including taking steps to put high-tech devices in the hands of those who need them most.

Of course, when addressing some issues, such as drugs or smoking, it's easy to see the clear objectives and sentiments you should be sharing kids. Case in point: Telling children not do drugs or smoke cigarettes is a simple, straightforward message with rapidly communicable benefits, and one that can be measured through the use of very tangible and attainable benchmarks. But with a more amorphous concept such as Digital Citizenship, which promotes positive behavior for a variety of reasons ranging from safety to enhancing career potential, stressing the need to be good online, and gauging how well the message has been received, can be a bit more ephemeral.

To help address these concerns, FOSI implemented a program to help put the concept into action. In partnership with Facebook, Google and a host of other major technology providers, FOSI now provides a Good Digital Parenting resource online where parents, teachers, kids and teens "can connect, share, and do good."

Those who sign up are essentially encouraged to share their positive online experiences and spread word about these stories, as well as learn the latest information and insights from the world of digital citizenship. There's an element of online volunteering included within the program as well, and all activity is easily shareable and able to be transmitted via social networks and other forms of electronic communication. In a way, A Platform for Good provides a different and more positive type of social networking experience, and one that experts from all walks of life can truly get behind. "All too often, online safety discussions focus on the dangers of technology," says Stephen Balkam, CEO of FOSI. "It's time to transform the discussion and create resources to inform, inspire and empower kids to make the right choices online."

Case in point: Benni Cinkle, founder of the That Girl in Pink Foundation, was once a victim of cyberharassment,

ridicule and bullying after a viral video featuring her awkwardly dancing catapulted her into the Internet limelight. Cinkle met the deluge of comments and criticism head-on though, eventually building a positive reputation as a trusted resource for advice for other teens facing bullying or other online issues. She recently authored a guest post in which she shares her secret – that it's actually "pretty easy to build a positive reputation online when you treat everything from posting pictures and updates, to responding to the things that people say about you, good and bad as if there wasn't a computer and Internet connection separating you from the rest of the world."

Among Cinkle's key tips for practicing good digital citizenship is her suggestion that teens leave the Internet a nicer place than when they found it. "Making a friend online by leaving a positive comment on a picture of someone you don't know or even just hitting the "Like" button to show them some love is an easy and quick way to lift someone's spirits," Cinkle says. These positive behaviors can turn a conversation away from those hoping to take it to a negative place, and continued positivity can even help you earn respect and credibility as a positive force for good online.

There are also a number of resources available for parents and teachers hoping to teach kids more about digital citizenship online, such as a free curriculum for elementary, middle and high schools at Common Sense Media. This program was developed by leaders in the field and promises "to help educators empower their students and their school communities to be safe, responsible, and savvy." A number of online games are also designed to be educational and fun for kids while teaching them ways to be good citizens online. NetSmartzKids is aimed at elementary-aged children, and uses cartoonish and colorful characters to star in games and videos teaching concepts of digital citizenship. Professor Garfield's Learning Lab likewise teaches kids lessons about cyberbullying, self-esteem, peer pressure and more.

TIPS FOR PARENTS

For those looking to practice good digital citizenship habits or immediately apply these principles, here are a few tips that can also help you get you started.

Do Unto Others... – Practice the golden rule of social media: Only post about others as you would have them post about you. Don't tag, belittle or share information you wouldn't want tagged, belittled or shared. Remember the golden rule, and always apply it to your online interactions, especially on social networking sites: Treat others the way you'd like to be treated, with respect, dignity and extra attention to how thoughts and actions will affect others. Putting yourself in other people's shoes

is a great way to make sure you're practicing positive digital citizenship.

The Grandma Rule – Before publicly sending any post, message, or update out into the online world, consider whether or not you'd want your grandma to see it. Because when you post something to a social network or send it directly to a friend, you've essentially lost all control – and it's theoretically possible it could make it into anyone (including your grandmother's) hands. Knowing that she's got enough gray hairs already without your added help, it pays to make sure that everything you do or say online is fit for her consumption. Remembering this rule can help keep kids from sharing inappropriate content or engaging in activities they otherwise shouldn't be.

Spread Heart, Not Hurt – With a tip of the hat to Yahoo! Safely and Common Sense for the perfect turn of a phrase, we love the idea of this simple slogan, a great way for kids to remember to spread and embrace positive messages, and avoid engaging in negative behavior. Share uplifting thoughts, words of love, and positive reinforcement, and you'll watch your social network connections, relationships and overall enjoyment grow exponentially.

Get the Lay of the Land–– Just as many experts recommend renting in a new area of the country before figuring out where to buy a home, it's good to approach social networks with a similar mentality. Each service has its own rules of conduct, methods of interaction and way of doing things, as well as accepted social norms. Before jumping right in, take a step back and observe how interactions take place, so you can decipher any unwritten rules or best practices for posting and sharing.

Respect Creativity – Even though it's easy to cut and paste another's work and pass it off as your creation, it's unfair and inappropriate to claim others' creative efforts as your own. Give credit where due if you are borrowing information or spreading someone else's message, anddon't plagiarize works or attempt to claim ownership of work in which you had no part of creating.

Be the Boss – Nobody can make you do anything you don't want to on social networks. Don't accept friend requests from people you don't know, don't let friends tag you when you don't want to be tagged, and don't respond to messages just because someone sent them to you. You are the one in charge – act like it, and you'll find it easier to manage the tone and type of online interactions encountered.

Remember the Three Ps of Information – All the information you share is permanent, public and powerful. Information is permanent because once you post it, the material can live online forever, even if you delete it off your profile. It's public because everyone can

potentially see it. And, of course, it's also powerful, as words and online actions can have a deep and lasting impact... so be sure that you're using them for good.

Privacy Settings – Use privacy settings to limit your posts to be visible only to those you really wish to see them. And even if you think you have your privacy setting completely locked down, assume that everything can and may potentially be seen others. Security breaches even on networks that are seemingly safe are more and more common these days – it never hurts to be paranoid here, and take a few added safety precautions. Or, for that matter, remember the best one of all: If material is risqué, controversial, highly personal, unpleasant in nature, has the potential to be misconstrued or misinterpreted, and/or you're not sure whether to share it, be smart, and don't post it at all.

PARENTING KIDS ON SOCIAL NETWORKS

Remember back when you were young, sitting in the back of the station wagon with your friends or siblings (facing backwards, of course), and you all were holding your own portable media player and playing GPS-enabled augmented reality apps or watching thousands of streaming videos? What about when you bought that new dragon action figure and you could take it over to your friend's house and watch it come to life as a 3D video game character? Or how about the time you were able to send instantaneous notes to any of your middle school classmates at all hours of the day, even in the middle of history lessons when no one was looking?

Of course you don't remember doing any of these things, because once upon a time (i.e. just 10 years ago), most were still the stuff of dreams or science fiction. But now, thanks to the explosion of connected mobile devices such as smartphones and tablets, and rise of popular online services like Webkinz, these high-tech fantasies have actually become reality for entire generations of children. So what's a parent to do in the modern era, when much of their childhood frames of reference are often irrelevant and their instincts are befuddled by ongoing technology overload? Only one thing's certain: You can't bury your head in the sand, with online-enabled technology devices and social networks by now well-ensconced in both contemporary households and the mainstream consciousness, and therefore permanently here to say.

As responsible parents and educators we must change with the times, so we must begin by educating ourselves surrounding the way in which social networks have impacted the very way in which children communicate. For example, while it may seem obvious to some, it may also comeas a surprise to others to learn: Adults and kids use Facebook very differently. While adults are very tuned into accepting friend requests from only those that they truly know and trust, kids are far more likely to use the service to connect to other children that they barely know. Similarly, while for many parents and adults the appeal to a service like Facebook is the sheer number of connections they have, for a kid that's sometimes a big turn off. We've talked to more than a few tweens and teens who are on Facebook because all their friends are, but that tell us they don't like to update or "use" it for the exact same reason — because it's passé, and so many friends are already on it. So they're constantly searching for other services which allow them to connect to the friends they want to in other, more novel and exciting ways.

Often, kids' unspoken rules involve finding ways to use Facebook how they want to despite the fact they're connected to you. There are detailed instructions easily accessible via Google and other search engines that offer kids tips on "how to friend your parents without sacrificing your privacy," which essentially serve as step-by-step guides for children on how to set up their privacy controls before accepting your friend request so that they can continue to post information without you seeing it, even if you're friends. According to one recent survey in fact, 80% of teens have admitted to posting content to Facebook that they've hidden from certain friends and/or parents by using privacy settings. So be aware that just because you're connected doesn't mean you'll see anything. In fact, a post being hidden from parents is what led to one notable incident in which a Texas Dad shot his daughter's laptop on a YouTube video in order to teach her a lesson. Although you may not agree with his tactic, this incident provides a great conversation point for you and your teens to explore differing opinions about what constitutes appropriate behavior online, and how parents should deal with inappropriate activities.

In a way, being on social networks is just like being out in public, except that there's a permanent record of everything you're doing out there being kept, and it all could come back to haunt you someday. Consider that you'd teach your kids proper manners and etiquette before taking them out to a restaurant, and teach them not to scream or throw fits at the table. Similarly, you need to make sure that your kids understand the basics and key issues before setting them free on social networks. Remember, there's pretty much no taking social networking off the table after it's been put up for grabs. Once introduced, there will be virtually no chance of getting kids off social networks. So before handing over the keys to them, realize that proper training and education is vital, and that making the connection may potentially expose children to individuals, interactions and influences viewed as negative or inappropriate by your family. Needless to say, it's crucial to provide proper training and insight up-front, and monitor their online activities accordingly, once social networks have been introduced.

TIPS FOR PARENTS

Cultivate Community Support – The reality is that families everywhere are facing tough digital decisions when it comes to parenting their kids on social networks. Questions wait at every turn, such as when's the best age to let them start connecting, how to ensure they're staying safe online, and what constitutes normal and appropriate online interaction. Alas, answers can be hard to come by, and differ by household – so make a point to talk to other parents about your feelings on these issues and to find out theirs, as many will be facing similar issues. Chances are, by doing so, you can suss out some great tips and learn a bit about what kids are dealing with these days. Oftentimes children will open up more to their friends about what's going on, who will then wind up sharing details with their parents. In either case, don't be afraid to lean on friends and peers for support. And don't forget to talk to your children's teachers, too. They're often at the frontlines of the latest trends that kids are obsessed with and talking about, and what social networks they're using, and may be just as attuned to many of the day-to-day issues being faced at school or otherwise.

Establish Family Guidelines – Just like every kid is different, every family is different, so take charge and set ground rules regarding technology and social media use that are right for your household. Start by considering screen time limits. To begin with, determine what counts as screen time: Is it just TV watching and computer time? Do smartphones and tablets count? What about using the PC to help with homework assignments?

Whatever your feeling, where possible, keeping computers in common areas and making sure you can see the screen of any device being used as needed can aid with the tracking process, though it's important to recall that children can and often will find alternate ways to access the Internet. In any case, establish the difference between what's a need and what's a privilege when it comes to screen time use. When setting time limits, consider beginning with a baseline allotment like 60 minutes a day of screen time, and adding or subtracting time based as a reward or punishment for good or bad behavior. With regard to social network usage, come up with a timer or other way to track the length and frequency of kids' online activities. It's easy to whittle away the hours checking out photos or interacting with friends, time which often is supposed to be used for more important tasks, like sports, homework, real-life activities or face-to-face interactions.

Likewise, talk about rules for social network usage as well as content that may be consumed upon these services (including thinking about movie, music and video game ratings) to determine where you'll draw the line for your family. It's imperative to have these conversations, and to continue to have them as kids grow older, as these ground rules will establish key building blocks for choices governing all your family's online and digital media consumption going forward. The decision to monitor your kids' Facebook accounts and how to do so are only part of the choices which must be made here – you must also figure out how often you'll be checking in. In a TRUSTe survey, 72% of parents surveyed said they monitor their teens' accounts, with 50% of these parents monitoring weekly, 35% daily and 10% monthly. Figure out what's right for your family, and have an open and honest discussion with your teens about how you'll be checking in.

Accentuate the Positive – While a decade ago horrified parents were beside themselves at the prospective horror of online predators stalking chatrooms looking for their next victims, the reality is that most kids are exposed to perfectly appropriate behavior most of the time. Likewise, instead of always focusing solely on the potential pitfalls of Internet usage or bad apples in terms of online users, it's important to help frequently educate children on the positive aspects of how social networks can enhance their lives as well.

As just one example, you'll want to teach kids the virtues of positive Digital Citizenship, the ability to apply real-life morals and judgments to online activities. While issues such as cyberbullying, identity theft and cybercrimes are real threats, and among the concerns children should be educated about online, they're not the be-all, end-all of the Internet experience. In fact, the real value in providing teaching and training around online interaction comes in educating kids how to appropriately act, and to know how to react if they ever do happen to encounter negative behaviors.

Teach kids to avoid controversial subjects or matters, and put others first. Nobody likes someone who only talks about themselves in real life, so teach children how to have a genuine interest in the activities of others, and to provide positive encouragement to these third parties as well. These real-life social skills translate great to the real-life networking world as well. Along similar lines, show your kids how to use social networks for more than just silly status updates and banal comments. Help them connect with others while studying, or to explore and discuss subject areas of interest.

Get Connected – Find out what social networks your kids are using, and if you're not already using them, you need to start, or at the very least have a firm understanding of how they work and how kids can use them. As a benefit, doing so may also provide some common ground for discussions with your teens at a time when having conversations that involve more than grunts or talking about how they're hungry can be rare and precious occasions. Tell your teens they don't need to be afraid to connect with you. Remind them that you don't want to interfere with or embarrass them, you just want to make sure they're making good choices, just like in real life. And even though kids may want to "hide" things they're posting from parents, the reality is that in today's world once information is made available, it's out there forever. So forcing kids to have a confirming thought of "do I want my mom to see this?" prior to posting anything actually isn't a bad thing.

Know Your Boundaries – Although we do recommend that you connect with your kids on Facebook, Twitter, Google+ or any other social network they may be on, you as a parent need to also know your boundaries, just as you do in real life. Just as you wouldn't rush the soccer field or take out the other team's goalie just to help your child score a goal, don't feel compelled to interject yourself into their online interactions and happenings. Refrain from posting to their wall on Facebook, and don't follow their friends on Facebook. One good alternative is to use social networks to connect to your kids' friends' parents. It's another great way to foster community connections and create a sense of safety around kids' activity.

Nurture Other Interests – If you are afraid your child is spending too much time online, help them find other outlets for their energy. Even if they're not into sports and activities, chances are there that there's some sort of crafty, artistic or other leisure-time outlet that they'll embrace, and it's up to you to help them track it down. Encourage your kid to spend at least 1.5-2X as much time as is spent online, if not several times more, engaged in real-life activities and hobbies. Whether simply requiring certain conversations to take place via phone or in person, or setting aside specific time for activities not related to online interaction, experts agree that a healthy balance between online time spent on social networks and other normal real-world activities is essential for kids to enjoy a healthy and balanced lifestyle. When kids are on social networks, and their real-life friends are online as well, consider encouraging them to connect more in the actual world.

Capitalize on Together Time When You Can – While you should keep at arm's length from certain online activities your kids enjoy with their friends, don't be afraid to use technology as a tool to help bring your family closer together as well. As an example, you might try playing video games with your kids on social networks, or watching video clips about subjects of shared interest. Not only will this help keep you up to speed on some of the activities your kids are enjoying on social networks. It's also an invaluable chance to connect with your kids on their turf, and can provide great perspective into their thoughts and opinions about all sorts of issues, not just on the specific game or movie you're playing.

Control Privacy Settings – Don't assume that everything is automatically configured just how you want it with your social network account from the get-go. Login and make sure all your updates, photos and more are visible only to those you know on Facebook, and consider setting up a family group to allow members of your household to share information amongst each other without broadcasting it to everyone else. If you're feeling overwhelmed, don't be afraid to turn to the service's help section for insights. Most popular social networks have extensive, easy–to–understand and searchable help sections too, so if you don't know how to perform a task (i.e. limiting who can see status updates), you can look up how to perform the function pretty easily.

Engage in Real-Life Dialogue – Talk to your kids about social networks. Whether you're discussing unique updates or articles you've spotted or chatting about general feelings about the service and current events, using the social network as a starting point can lead to great conversations with your kids. Norton Safety Expert Marian Merritt says it's important for parents to have these conversations with children and to establish a dialogue of trust from an early age. "Make sure to talk to them about being comfortable enough to come talk to you when they have any questions or if they are confronted with something online that makes them feel uncomfortable," advises Merritt. Part of establishing that level of comfort starts with being able to have comfortable and casual, everyday conversations with your children around technology – not just the troubling parts.

Avoid Negative Situations – It's not nice to talk about people behind their backs, and many families also operate by the old saying "if you can't say anything nice, don't say anything at all." So make sure your kids understand not to engage in negative banter about others, and not to post pictures of them that they wouldn't want posted of themselves. Likewise, they'll want to avoid saying anything negative about specific people, places, co–workers or bosses. It's likely that anything said on a social network would find its way back to them, and could lead to some negative consequence such as an argument, the loss of a job, or the loss of privileges.

Keep Tomorrow in Mind – Although no one knows exactly what the future holds, chances are your kids will be applying to college after high school, and soon after that entering the workforce. In the future, those making life–changing decisions about your child's career are sure to examine their social media profiles in addition to any other information they've made public. So remind kids that the things they post now can and likely will be used against them, even if it's five or ten years down the line.

MORE BASIC TIPS FOR KIDS STARTING OUT ON SOCIAL NETWORKS:

• Remember to log out of all accounts and networks after using them, especially if you're on a computer or device that will be used by others.

• When asking someone you only marginally know to be your friend, send a short message explaining who you are and why you're attempting to contact them.

• Make sure you understand the site's chat or contact options, how to use them, and who you'll be able to send and receive messages from.

• Use your real birth year (not necessarily birthday, if you'd like to protect your privacy) when registering. There's no reason to lie, and networks tailor certain parts of their services – e.g. what content or material you can access – based on your real age.

• For parents, make sure you use the parental controls provided on each social network service, usually in the form of a "parent dashboard." Not only can you tweak privacy settings here, but you'll also be able to review activity logs from the time your child spends online.

WHAT AGE IS A GOOD AGE TO GET STARTED?

Due to COPPA requirements, major social networks all have policies in place within their terms of service that prohibit users under the age of 13 from signing up for service. However, the reality is that many parents help their kids setup social network accounts long before their 13th birthday.

While we don't always recommend this, with proper parental supervision and a firm understanding of how, why and when children will be using these services, it's possible that there are some circumstances where certain households may wish to allow kids 12 and under to join social networks if they want to connect with relatives and/or use them on a limited scale. Nonetheless, most experts do recommend kids be a least 13 years of age before they are set out on their own on social networks, free to connect and share with others. Parental involvement and monitoring is obviously still warranted, though.

For those hoping to skirt the debate entirely while giving kids a chance to get comfortable with communicating online, it may help to note that there are also social networks geared for kids 12 and under. Designed to be fully compliant with COPPA privacy laws, many provide great choices for children looking to connect with friends to share ideas and reviews. Here's a look at a few:

Club Penguin – Offered by Disney, Club Penguin is a social network parents can trust, with kids taking on a penguin avatar and playing fun games and other activities while connecting with others.

EdModo – Designed for use by teachers and classes, EdModo provides a place to connect and collaborate on projects and homework or just enjoy general discussion.

Fanlala – Aimed at tween fans of tween and teen celebrity, Fanlala creates communities around well-known personalities, inviting kids to connect with other fans with similar interests.

Fantage – Fantage is a virtual world in which kids use an avatar to mix, mingle and play games that are designed to be educational and fun.

KidzBop – Parents may be familiar with the KidzBop music series, but this social network is from the same folks, and invites children to login and connect with others and share their passions for music and other entertainment.

KidzVuz – KidzVuz is a place where kids can create video reviews of their favorite products and share them with others while viewing other video reviews of products they like or are interested in.

KidzWorld –Offering free games, moderated chat and news stories on events and topics that are interesting for kids, KidzWorld is an ad-supported gathering place where children can discuss pop culture.

SkiddyKids – Aimed at girls between ages 6 and 14, it's designed to give kids the social network experience while also providing activities like games and movies that they enjoy. There's also a book club, toy exchange and even moderated and regulated Twitter and YouTube functionality.

SweetyHigh – Billing itself as a social game for girls, SweetyHigh lets teens earn real-life rewards and prizes for their participation in the virtual school.

Webkinz – Webkinz provide a real-world toy that can be transferred online and used as virtual toy to play in and explore an online world populated by other kids playing as their Webkinz.

YourSphere is designed for kids 18 and under and subjects its applicants to strict background checks, and features games, activities and a system for earning credits.

MONITORING YOUR KIDS ONLINE

While we recommend fostering ongoing conversation and open dialogue about social network usage, part of responsible household maintenance involves checking up on kids and their activities periodically. To this extent, part of your family's Internet agreement should also specify the need for regular check-ins, the use of monitoring software, and the importance of having access to records or feedback on all children's activities and searches, where humanly possible. By all means, make a point of being up-front with your kids about this plan, as you don't want them to think you are spying on them without their knowledge. Moreover, many times simply recognizing that one's parents will be keeping an ongoing eye on their activities is enough of a deterrent to keep kids from engaging in pursuits they shouldn't.

Of course, there are also certain instances – such as when harassment, cyberbullying and issues with inappropriate behavior are involved – that may require parents to access kids' social networks without permission or advance notice. If you do find yourself forced to take this step, don't be afraid to explain to your kids why you thought the situation was serious enough to warrant the intrusion, as you'll want to promote education and empathy, and maintain their trust, even after the incident. Even though many computers and web browsers come with some monitoring features built in, we recommend checking out the following additional programs that provide monitoring and other safeguards. All can help better provide peace of mind, and ensure that kids have a more positive online experience.

WebWatcher – www.webwatcherkids.com – WebWatcher bills itself as an online chaperone, and encourages users to

think of the service as a parenting tool. It serves not only as a safeguard against inappropriate sites, but records Internet and general computer usage, giving parents the option to block access to specific websites or activities based on their children's behavior. Be aware though, that access comes with a cost attached.

Net Nanny – www.netnanny.com – As one of the best-known brands in terms of parental control and monitoring software, NetNanny not only allows for tracking and viewing of kids' online activity across all popular social networks, but also provides tools that offer more positive and healthy Internet experiences for kids. Utilizing NetNanny's timers, filters and inappropriate content blockers helps parents have peace of mind that are kids are protected from more than the dangers they're finding on their own as part ofpersonal monitoring efforts. There's also a version for mobile devices, too – an Android version is currently available, and an iOS version is coming soon. NetNanny comes with an annual fee per year per computer and mobile device attached.

Cybersitter – www.cybersitter.com – Cybersitter offers a great value for families, with the ability to install the service on up to three computers for a relatively low cost. You can create your own custom block and allow lists, record e-mails and Facebook activity, and also set certain times when specific sites can be accessed (and when they can't). Some of the controls and features require parents to be more computer literate than the average user, but if you're simply trying to keep up with your kid's activity online, you may need to be willing to expand your tech-savviness already.

Norton Online Family – onlinefamily.norton.com – The Norton Online Family suite of products allows families to set time limits, filter web content and receive reports and summaries of online usage and activity. While the full range of services costs a small amount each year, there's also a free version which provides basic monitoring and limiting capabilities. If you're looking for a great way to start monitoring or to get a feel for the process, Norton Online Family is a great option.

Mobicip – www.Mobicip.com – Mobicip has emerged as a leader in smartphone monitoring and web filtering efforts, allowing for a broad range of blocking/filtering options and parental controls, all of which can apply to all your family's mobile devices. Better yet, settings can be easily tweaked from a computer. Mobicip offers online reports of activity and time logs, and can also send these out via scheduled e-mail alerts. Basic filtering is available for a low one-time fee, and the full suite of features costs a minor amount per year on top of that.

McAfee Family Protection – Designed to protect children of all ages from exposure to inappropriate content, strangers and social network risks, McAfee Family Protection provides a wide range of filtering and parental control functions, including activity reports providing a view of all Internet and IM activity that your kids are doing.

Online Guardian – From the security and monitoring experts at Trend Micro, Online Guardian for Families monitors Internet activity around the clock, tracking web browsing history, wall posting, messags, photos and chats. The program allows filtering as well as time limits, to help manage the entire online experience.

uKnowKids – This dashboard is designed specifically to make it easy to monitor your kids' social network activities, compiling Facebook, Twitter and Instragram into a streamlined feed so you can see everything in one place. uKnowKids also collects text messages, contacts, images, apps, check-ins and location histories so you can see what's happening at a glance.

MANAGING YOUR ONLINE REPUTATION

Have you Googled yourself lately? How about your kids? It's entirely possible you're not doing it often enough, as a recent report showed that less than half of us did so regularly. However, chances are someone else is looking you up in online searches already. Whether it's a current or former classmate, college recruiter, prospective employer, or someone your family just met, looking up information about others online is one of the first steps many people take when trying to learn more about them. Alas, the information they find may not always be flattering, accurate or representative of one's character. Worse, even if you know the information out there is inaccurate, it doesn't always matter, because we cannot always control what appears in search results and, as the saying goes, perception is reality.

The Digital Tattoo Project, funded by the University of British Columbia's teaching and learning enhancement fund, likens one's digital footprint to a tattoo. This is a great analogy, because not only does it encompass the unique artistic expressions we all favor, but it perfectly reflects the permanence of information which appears online. Moreover, the concept likewise captures the essence and feel of what it's like to live the rest of your life with the consequences of decisions and updates you make when you're younger and less wise or

experienced. It's therefore imperative that you use any resources you can to stay on top of your family's digital image and learn how to protect your online reputation, which tends to linger – and not always for the positive.

According to a recent report from Kaplan Test Prep, college admissions officers' use of Facebook to learn more about potential applicants has quadrupled, and is continuing to grow. According to the report, 24% of admissions officials say they used social networks to check on prospective students, up from 6% the previous year, and 20% used Google to help evaluate an applicant. In short, what kids say, do and share online will absolutely have a lasting impact on their future.

A recent infographic from KBSD Digital Marketing likewise shows that 78% of job recruiters check search engines when researching potential employees and half of recruiters and HR professionals refer to personal websites when deciding whether or not to hire you. They're looking at the information, photos and videos you post, hoping to find positive feedback and reinforcement for making hiring decisions, but all too often encountering unflattering or even incriminating information.

Using Facebook and similar social networks effectively allows colleges and potential employers to obtain information they won't find on potential candidates as part of the routine application process. The good news is that that the number of admissions or hirings that have been "negatively impacted" by these checks is actually on the decline. However, the bad news is that still nearly one in ten applicants are being rejected for the use of vulgarity, or engaging in underage drinking, inappropriate behavior and even plagiarism, with infractions found courtesy of unwise postings on social networking sites.

Wondering what media or information is floating around out there with your name, face or image attached? The Digital Tattoo Project recommends using sites like pipl.com to find out what comes up about yourself across a broad range of social networks. Other services and sites such as spezify also provide handy visual representations of one's online identity, helping illustrate the overall perceptions you're creating online.

Looking to better control the message you're sending to the world at large? Here are some basic tips to help you control your image while still maintaining a positive online presence:

Consider Your Online Footprint: Realize that everything you post or any picture that appears of you online may be available for public viewing. There are many who refuse to ever have a photo taken of themselves holding an alcoholic drink, let alone share it on the Internet or social networks, for example. Note that although you can lock down Facebook and Google+ privacy settings, if you're on Twitter, be aware that anything you tweet is easily searchable as well, so be leery of taking any potentially controversially viewpoints or stands.

Use Common Sense: In addition to not posting personal or potentially controversial information, never share material that casts you in an unflattering light, doing anything illegal or unethical, or engaging in risqué pursuits, pranks, or other ill-advised actions. Likewise, stay positive, and keep snide remarks to a minimum – negativity never plays well in others' eyes, online or otherwise. Also make a point of disabling settings within social networks that allow you to be tagged by others. Ultimately, stay in control of your own information, and be smart about what you do share.

Focus on Positive Networking: Take steps to help kids create their own personal brand by highlighting activities and thought leadership in areas they want to be associated with. For example, if they want people to see them as someone who appreciates the arts, have them ask questions about or post information from art classes or school concerts. You'll be surprised how quickly you can change others' perceptions by focusing your observations and sharing on specific areas of interest.

Control Your Information: Take advantage of privacy settings wherever you can. Don't expect a social network or photo sharing service to preconfigure default settings exactly how you want them. If your kids will be posting information or sharing photos that you (or they) would never want the public at large or college recruiters and/or future prospective employers to see, make sure to restrict access to their accounts and content.

Don't Overshare: Just as you enjoy reading updates from others, they also enjoy hearing from you, but there's clearly a line that can and often does get crossed when it comes to sharing too much, or too much information. Instead of passing along every funny pet picture you stumble across or article about your sports team, filter yourself and only share this type of information once every couple of days to avoid bombarding contacts. Your friends will appreciate not being pounded with a deluge of updates and will instead look forward to the times you do post (especially when sharing items of greater weight and import), which will also lead to more meaningful exchanges and interactions.

Spread Positive Messages: Kids need to be empowered to realize that they can shape their own image on social networks, and utilize these services in positive ways. Once they're using social networks, these platforms can also serve as amplifiers for the information your kids decide to share, helping spread messages far and wide – much to the world's benefit. Facebook spokesperson Marian Heath says that she hears from people all the time that Facebook is a place where there kids can get into trouble. But she also urges parents and teens to turn the issue around, because it doesn't have to be that way." You can build your own image online," Heath says. "Post the good things you're doing and share your interests. Have conversations so folks can find out what's interesting to you. Ask friends about books you're reading, plays you're interested in." In other words, instead of focusing on negative or gossipy aspects of social networking exchanges, think about how you can use these services to do good, have fun, and shape your online image more appropriately.

Know What's Out There: Research yourself on a variety of search engines to see what pops up, and pretend that you are someone who knows nothing about you and see what kind of info they'll find. Consider what appears on the first few pages of search results, how it reflects upon you, and make sure to consider what images, videos and other assets are out there associated with your name. If you do find yourself in a situation where there is information or media available online about you or your family that you'd rather wasn't out there, you may wish to consider using one of these services to help manage your online reputation:

Reputation.com offers free scans to help you find information online, with an option to subscribe to help keep your reputation clean. Be forewarned though: For those that do have information they want to remove, costs to get that info removed or changed can quickly add up, with it being even more expensive if you have a common name. BrandYourself helps make entries you want to highlight more visible in search results than those you may want removed. The service attempts to make the process much simpler and user-based than rivals, offering "do-it-yourself" tips and free profiling and alerts. The free version of the platform will help optimize up to three links and track the first page of Google search results for your name. For a recurring fee per month, you can also boost your plan to unlimited links and track the first 10 pages of results.

Integrity Defenders helps individuals or businesses remove negative comments or content from the first page of search results on the most popular search engines like Google, Bing and Yahoo! for a set price, and even offers to push the content off the first and second pages for twice that cost.

For those interested in reading more on reputation management, Microsoft also offers a number of tipsand helpful online resources to help you take control of your online image.

Unfriending: As important as it is to positively manage friend requests on social networks, it's also important to know how and when to defriend unwanted parties. Some sites, i.e. Facebook, allow for the option to quietly de-friend others without notification, or to simply ignore a friend request in perpetuity. Other networks like Twitter allow for complete blocking of other users, meaning they can no longer follow or communicate with you through the service.

When should you unfriend someone? If they're engaging in disruptive, harmful behavior, or taking away from your enjoyment of social networks, it's okay to cut the virtual cord. Although it's likely no one will ever notice when this action has been taken, especially if you're discrete, help your kids consider what to say should friends ask them about it. If there are specific examples of inappropriate behavior or infractions that they can point to, then great, but otherwise they may consider simply pointing to the fact that they're trying to keep their networks to a manageable size.

WHAT'S OK TO SHARE ON SOCIAL NETWORKS – AND HOW TO SHARE IT?

Wondering what's safe to share with friends, family and the general public via social media? Unfortunately, rules of proper online conduct can be somewhat murky, and may differ between individual and network. Luckily for those looking to become better communicators, the following expert hints and tips – excerpted from high-tech etiquette guide Netiquette Essentials: New Rules for Minding Your Manners in a Digital World – can help shed some light on the matter.

• Sharing extremely-opinionated viewpoints (e.g. political leanings or thoughts on controversial topics) can be a lightning rod online. Think twice before liking supporting status updates or posting such opinions, which can incite and aggravate others (and live on in perpetuity). If you feel the need to express these opinions, consider confining such communications to exchanges with individual friends, or specific Facebook or Google+ groups. Ultimately though, it's important to remember: If you don't have anything nice to say, perhaps it's best left unsaid.

• Posting embarrassing, revealing or negative photos of yourself should be avoided at all costs. Remember: Images you share may be taken at face value, and/or viewed as representative of your character – not to mention live on for forever on the Internet. What seems cute in high school or college may not seem quite so endearing to potential employers.

• Never post photos of others without their express permission.

• Relationship or personal drama is best kept private. If you cannot resist the urge to share, do so sparingly – and in the most vague, unspecific terms possible – for the sake of involved parties, or friends uninterested or unwilling to participate in the situation. No communications should be shared about other individuals and those involved in real-life situations without their advance permission.

• As a rule of thumb, uncomfortable or revealing personal information, i.e. details of your struggles with psychological issues or relatives' fading health, should be shared sparingly, if at all, and – unless acquaintances have indicated that they're comfortable viewing this content – only with others you know in real-life. Note that content shared online may further be available for public viewing, and inadvertently expose you or your family to potential risk and/or embarrassment.

• Never share intimate personal details including birthdates, phone numbers, addresses, schools or hometowns online, to minimize risks of crime, vandalism or identity theft. Never let others know when you'll be away from your home, especially for any given length of time, e.g. while on vacation.

• Avoid posting on social networks unless you have a tight grasp over your privacy settings, and are completely comfortable with the group of online friends that your updates will be shared with.

• Professionalism is imperative – if you wouldn't say it in a social or work setting, don't say it online, in the most public of forums.

• Politeness and respect are vital: Always be considerate of others, and treat them the way that you'd wish to be treated.

• Avoid bad-mouthing other users as it will negatively impact your image and casual bystanders may judge you based on these actions.

• Maintain a positive tone and attitude: Negativity, complaints and condescending messages often reflect poorly on the poster.

• Bragging and self-aggrandizing statements should be avoided, and making them may cause you to lose friends and followers.

• Since social networks are shared venues enjoyed in mixed company, always avoid using vulgar language and making derogatory remarks.

• Demanding that others share your status updates, projects, thoughts or ideas is inappropriate.

• Reserve confidential discussions for private message threads or, better yet, phone calls, emails or other venues where interactions aren't recorded in perpetuity online.

• Be advised that conversational nuances and subtle shifts in tone or personality may be lost in translation, and that individual users may interpret messages differently: Consider how posts will be read and interpreted before sending.

• Poor spelling, punctuation, grammar and choice of words can reflect equally poorly upon the individual – proofread all communications before sending. Shorthand, abbreviations and online slang should be avoided if possible, and used only in the most informal of conversations.

REFERENCE GUIDE: POPULAR SOCIAL NETWORKS

FACEBOOK

What It Is: After a February 2004 debut, Facebook slowly evolved from a student-only network centered around Harvard and Boston to the most popular website in the world (behind Google), engaging nearly half of the US population and more than a billion users worldwide. The company went public in 2012, and continues to expand and grow, acquiring popular services like Instagram while constantly tweaking its interface and offerings. This perpetual tinkering is actually an important point to consider when looking at what's effectively the great granddaddy of all social networks. Facebook is constantly changing so much that it's best to focus on best practices with regard to appropriate social network behavior and usage instead of specific features and functionalities, which are consistently changing. For more on specific updates and tips, make sure to tune into www.AKeynoteSpeaker.com.

Who's Using It: There are more than 1.44 billion active Facebook users worldwide. More than three quarters of teens report being active on social networks – Facebook naturally being a primary port of call. In short, even if everybody isn't technically using Facebook, it certainly seems like it... odds are that the majority of individuals you know will be. Teens especially feel compelled to use it because of its popularity, even though they may show preferences for other services more.

Why Your Kids Will Want to Use It: Children use Facebook to connect with friends, chat, and share updates, photos, videos and links for a variety of reasons, such as to announce life achievements, plan get-togethers and simply unwind. Research has found that kids use Facebook as a complement to real-life relationships though, not as a substitute, so often the friends they interact with online are the same ones they interact with in real life.

Ways to Connect: Becoming connected on Facebook requires action on behalf of both parties. One must initiate a friend request, and the other must accept it. Experts agree and we recommend that kids should only "friend" people that they know on Facebook, although often kids will end up friending everyone in their class, even if they don't really know them on a personal basis.

Note that it is possible to defriend someone on Facebook, and this is something that either party can do. To remove a friend, simply visit their profile and click the unfriend link. If you do want to connect again, you'll need to go through the friend request process another time.

You can also block a user who you don't want to be visible to on Facebook. By doing this, you break all ties with them, and both users will no longer be able to see each other's profiles or appear in any search results. This process is a little more difficult to accomplish, but can be handled within privacy settings or via a link at the bottom of each profile.

Facebook has a few different privacy settings that users can control, and you can decide who is able to see and interact with your kids. The most restrictive setting is "Friends Only," which makes their information visible only to those who are on their Friends list. There's also a "Friends of Friends" option which makes updates visible to anyone that is connected to someone that is connected to you. (In other words, if this setting is enabled, then anyone that's friends with someone that your kid is friends with can see the information that they post on their profile, or at times in their news stream). And, of course, there is also a "Public" setting, which is often the default, which makes all posts visible to anyone who views your profile.

Facebook also provides extra settings for users who are between 13 and 17 to make sure their profiles and posts don't show up in public search results, and lets you restrict your audience for

location-sharing services to friends only. Once your child comments on a photo or friend's status update though, remember that this information is visible to anyone that the original poster is connected to.

Notable Points for Parents: As with coming to grips with any real world opportunity, once you join a social network like Facebook, it can take some time to get your sea legs and feel comfortable with how you're comporting yourself online. Worth considering here: As adults, we learn to tread lightly and cautiously before diving into activities, but kids are experiential learners and are often willing to dive right in to any new activity, heedless of potential drawbacks. Knowing this, it's important for parents to have a firm understanding of how Facebook works because kids can easily seek out and find ways to circumvent parental controls and hide updates from family members. It may seem like a daunting task, but you'll need to become a social networking expert to try and keep up with them – such are the perils of ever-changing technology.

On the bright side, to help you in this regard, here are some of the most commonly made mistakes by kids and grown-ups alike when using Facebook, and how to address them:

Overfriending – Anyone just getting started on social networks is likely to be met with a slew of potential connecting requests from friends and family once they join and make a few interactions. Etiquette with regards to friend requests is a delicate subject, and often kids will feel compelled to accept any invitations they receive, even if they don't really know who's sending them. From the moment they get on Facebook, remind kids that they are in control of their experience, and in order to keep that control, they need to ensure they're only connecting with folks who they recognize and wish to be synced up with. No one should ever be compelled to accept a request from a friend or passing acquaintance, and Facebook makes it easy to ignore requests.

Sharing Too Much Information – We've covered the dangers of sharing personal information or sensitive details of one's life on Facebook. But kids also have a tendency to overshare when engaging in conversations and connections, often participating in lengthy back-and-forth dialogues within the comments section of a post, available for the world to see. Teach your kids to keep conversations between one another private, or use Facebook's chat features or another IM (Instant Messaging) or texting program to facilitate them, so as to respect privacy and not inundate others' with pointless updates.

Misusing Apps and Games – While Facebook makes it very easy to enjoy games and other fun activities on its platform, there are a few things to be leery of should your children wish to engage in them. For starters, because these games use Facebook as a platform, many integrate posts, achievements, and sharing or purchase requests, which users are encouraged to post to their profiles, essentially providing free publicity for the apps. But the truth is most friends won't want to see these updates, so you need to make sure your kids know not to share them from within Facebook games and apps to minimize spam and clutter. Secondarily, such software programs are also often provided free of charge, but offer features that cost real-life money to enjoy. Facebook uses a payment system based on credits that are purchased using actual dollars and cents, which the titles can easily access and hope to entice users into tapping in order to buy in-app purchases (known as "microtransactions") – e.g. buying power-ups or access to new features in the favorite games. Any child enjoying apps or playing games on Facebook needs to understand the realities of how these titles operate, proper online shopping behavior, and your family's rules about buying virtual or real-world items online. Similarly, as a parent, you need to keep an eye out to make sure they're not racking up real-world bills in these virtual confines.

Failing to Educate Oneself – Homework isn't for kids alone. Get to know the social networks kids visit and spend some time having them show you how to interact with these sites and services.

Not only will you have a better understanding of exactly what they're doing as they're staring at the screen, but you'll also be forming memorable connections on "their turf" that will help you engender the necessary level of trust you may need as you look to guide and inform their ongoing digital life. You'll also have a better awareness of the kinds of conversations or exchanges you may be overhearing in the classroom or at home, and will be better prepared to address anything questionable that kids are discussing.

Overstepping One's Bounds – Getting to know Facebook, Instagram or Twitter ourselves and keeping abreast of children's online activity is important, but so is giving kids their space. Providing kids – especially younger tots – complete autonomy can be dangerous, but so can overcompensating, a common mistake that parents and teachers make. In short, try as much as you can to be an invisible, trusted guide to sprouts' online experiences, and be subtle where possible – but don't allow yourself to be entirely unaware. For example, if children misbehave or engage in behavior that's questionable, don't chastise them online, but rather bring the conversation to real life and deal with it there.

Not Considering that Kids Use Technology Differently – Just as most adults couldn't imagine sending more than 100 text messages a day, kids may not be able to wrap their heads around

why grown-ups would want to bother using their mobile device as a phone. Conversations are so awkward, in their opinion. Additionally, while social networks like Facebook are great for parents to connect with other friends and family, many kids use the service almost out of necessity, and seek out other, less public ways to communicate with friends. It's vitally important to recognize that children of every age group may use technology and online services uniquely – and oftentimes in ways vastly different to our own.

No Tech Empathy – It's tough to stop doing something you're right in the middle of, so be aware that kids who may be playing a game or engaging with friends in an online activity via social networks may find quitting immediately tricky to accomplish, especially if they're taking part in an involved interaction. Consider giving 5- or 10-minute warnings so kids know when they need to wrap up, and be sympathetic that they may want to reach an appropriate stopping point (e.g. a predetermined place where games can be exited and/or saved) before coming to dinner. By understanding a bit more about how and what technologies children are using, you'll be able to know whether they really need the extra two minutes to finish up a task, or whether they're pushing the limits of acceptable guidelines, in which case you need to reel them in.

Assuming Parental Controls Are Set the Right Way – The vast majority of parents and educators seem to think that just because a social network or network-ready device has parental controls built in that these safeguards are adequate to protect children out of the box. Wrong. Controls for every service, app, and device should be checked, set and customized to your family's settings – many are not configured, or configured to taste, by default. Restrict content, require passcodes and even set usage timers – devices provide a wide number of tools for parents and teachers, although few take the time to access and leverage all of them.

Modeling Bad Behavior – For parents specifically, if you don't want your kids to constantly be checking their social network profiles and phones at the dinner table or out at a restaurant, make sure you're not engaging in the same activities yourself. Words can only go so far, as kids often model actions and base their own high-tech interactions around how they see their parents interacting with technology. Treat your devices with respect and set limits for yourself, and your kids will have no problem doing the same.

HOW TO GET HELP FROM FACEBOOK

Although Facebook is fairly simple to utilize, many a parent has been stumped by how to get help or report issues via the service. While standard post, share and comment functions may be simple to grasp for social networking beginners, it's not always easy to comprehend or find how to utilize advanced functions.

To report anything concerns you might encounter on the service, simply visit www.Facebook.com/Report. Here, you'll find details on any form of activity that needs to be brought to the site's attention, all in one place. Families will also want to familiarize themselves with the Facebook Family Safety Center at www.Facebook.com/Safety. You'll find a ton of information there geared towards parents, kids, teachers, law enforcement officials and more, all designed to help users have a safe and positive online experience.

Lastly, here's one final tip for Facebook which may come in useful on a family road trip. If you or someone you know needs to use Facebook in a public place, you can request a one-time password to be used for logging into your account, provided you have a mobile number associated with said login. Simply text "otp" (as in one time password) to 32665 and you'll get a password that's good for 20 minutes.

LEARNING THE LINGO

You can find a full list of key Facebook vocabulary terms found within the site's Help Center Glossary, but here are a few key pieces of information and slang defined (Source: Facebook).

BANNER – Recently, Facebook changed the aesthetic of everyone's profile page. Now, people can select a large "banner" image, graphic or logo to best represent them which is prominently profiled on top of each timeline page.

BLOCK – You can block someone from seeing your profile, adding you as a friend, and sending you messages. Blocked also can mean that Facebook has temporarily restricted you from using a specific feature or multiple features, but you can still access your account.

CLICKJACKING – When you click on certain malicious websites, they may perform an action without your permission (ex: posting to your profile or timeline).

CREDITS – Credits are Facebook's virtual form of currency that you can use to engage with games and apps and make online purchases.

FRIEND – Friends are people you connect and share with on Facebook.

FRIENDSHIP – A friendship page shows a friendship history between two friends on Facebook. To try it, visit a friend's profile (timeline), open the gear menu in the top-right corner and select See Friendship.

GROUP – Groups are close circles of people that share and keep in touch on Facebook.

LIKE – Clicking "Like" is a way to give positive feedback and connect with things you care about.

LISTS – Lists are an optional way to organize your friends on Facebook.

MESSAGES – Messages is a central place to exchange private messages, chats, emails and mobile texts with friends.

NEWS FEED – Your news feed is the ongoing list of updates on your home page that shows you what's new with the friends and pages you follow.

NOTIFICATIONS – Notifications are email, onsite, or mobile updates about activity on Facebook.

PAGE – Pages allow businesses, brands, and celebrities to connect with people on Facebook. Admins can post information and news feed updates to people who like their page.

POKE – You can poke someone to get their attention or say hello. (Note: This is definitely one of the weirder and seemingly less useful parts of Facebook.)

PROFILE PICTURE – Your profile picture is the main photo of you on your profile (timeline). Your profile picture appears as a thumbnail next to your comments and other activities.

TAGGING – A tag links a person, page, or place to something you post, like a status update or a photo. For example, you can tag a photo to say who's in the photo or post a status update and say who you're with at the time of posting. A privacy setting called "Tag Review" helps you manage these.

TICKER – The Ticker, found on the right-hand side of your home page, lets you see all your friends' activity in real-time.

TIMELINE – Your timeline is your collection of photos, stories, and experiences that tell your story – e.g. your user profile.

TOP STORY – Your top stories are stories published since you last checked your news feed that Facebook thinks you'll find interesting. They're specifically marked and may be different depending on how long it's been since you last visited your news feed.

WALL – Your Wall is the space on your profile where you and friends can post and share.

As may be obvious by now, Facebook is the 800lb gorilla of the social media world. It's the social network that seemingly everyone knows about. It's free, easy-to-use and accessible from nearly any high-tech device with an Internet connection. The whole experience is streamlined, elegant and continues to beconstantly updated and refined.

This constant evolution is also one of the major sources of public complaint for Facebook, though. The interface and terms of service seem to be constantly changing, and it can be difficult for parents to keep up with everything that's going on around the platform. Facebook is large and ubiquitous enough that it's hard to imagine living in a world without it, however. Whether that means looking back and being thankful it wasn't around back when you were in high school, or looking forward and imagining what it will be like for students a decade hence, the fact is that Facebook seems to be the predominant face of social networking, and promises to stay that way for the foreseeable future.

As a company, Facebook takes concerns about privacy and online safety very seriously, even though the company often gets a lot of flack in the press for seemingly lackadaisical privacy settings and too frequent privacy changes. Facebook has a number of initiatives as a company that it either produces or promotes, such as partnerships with MTV, the Pager Center, Trend Micro and many other organizations and providers. The company also provides PSA videos with teen stars that will appeal to teens.

TWITTER

What It Is: Twitter is an online 'microblogging' network in which users can share and send short text messages, limited to 140 characters in length which can include access to pictures, videos and website links. Posts are all public and searchable unless a user chooses to make them private. Twitter encourages parents to engage with their kids about the practice of tweeting, as posting is known, even offering some helpful guidelines for doing so. The site suggests that kids ask themselves the following question before every tweet (i.e. post) that they send:

• Who are you sharing this information with?

• Can you trust all the people that see the information on your profile?

• How could your tweet be interpreted?

• Would you say what you are tweeting out loud or to a person's face?

While it may seem like everyone can follow anyone that these choose, there are some simple, basic safeguards in place to help protect one's privacy. Twitter also contains a feature that allows users to easily block other users, which can easily be accomplished from a drop down menu on a user's profile page, and ensures that this user is unable to follow or interact with you again. But Twitter does try play the role of Switzerland (a.k.a. neutral party) when it comes to user exchanges. The company considers itself a communications platform and not a content provider, so it doesn't mediate disputes between users. However, it does provide a link where users can report tweets that violate privacy or copyright concerns, or include instances of harassment, impersonation, reposting without attribution, child pornography and spam. The reporting hub page makes it possible to make administrators aware of any issues.

Who's Using It: Although Twitter has more than 500 million accounts, the latest statistics show that there are more than 300 million active Twitter users who tweet an average of 500 million tweets per day. The majority of Twitter users are between 18 and 49, with 84% falling in this age range. However, numerous tweens, teens and children make use of the service, which ranks second only to Facebook in mainstream awareness.

Why Your Kids Will Want to Use It: Children use Twitter to connect with friends for short text messaging-type exchanges, as well as to follow brief updates from celebrities and other well-known figures. Through the use of hashtags or content category markers (e.g. #movies, #music, #parenting etc.), kids will also enjoy participating in group discussions or topics with others worldwide. As a recent article in USA Today points out, many teens have actually flocked to Twitter because their parents and grandparents have all friended them on Facebook. And with the fast pace of communication on Twitter, they can interact with friends and others faster than grown-ups can keep up with. Twitter's usage among teens has actually doubled in a two–year span, and is only expected to continue to grow.

Ways to Connect: Following others is as simple as clicking a button on anyone from whom you'd like to hear more. The individual could be a friend, a celebrity, a local news outlet, or someone who just happens to tweet a lot about topics you are interested in. Bear in mind that following is not a two-way proposition – it only takes action on the part of the follower to be able to receive someone's tweets directly. There is a way that you as a parent can help restrict who follows you or your kids, though. Twitter offers a way to "protect" your tweets by making them private and asking you to approve anyone that wants to follow these messages. This setting also keeps your tweets out of public search results.

Notable Points for Parents: Twitter can be a tough service for parents and grandparents to wrap their head around. Let's start with the basics.

To begin with, each text update posted on Twitter is called a tweet and consists of no more than 140 characters. How

long is that? Consider that this paragraph is 179 characters long, and would be too long to be a tweet.

Needless to say, the size of messages aren't overwhelming, or even as large as many common sentences. So who can post and read tweets, or would want to? Anyone that signs up for an account can send a tweet. And each of those tweets can be viewed by anyone online, even if they don't have an account – sometimes, much of the fun is simply observing posts and reactions. And this is the point where Twitter can begin to feel overwhelming, especially from an ADD-deprived adult's perspective. But it's really not.

Happily, you never see all those tweets at once. If you have a Twitter account, you will only see in your timeline the most recent posts from those you have decided to follow. You'll also see a few "sponsored" tweets from companies that have paid money to place their message into everyone's timeline.

Searching is the other way that people view tweets. Twitter invites users to use the # symbol, called a hashtag, in front of words or phrases that may help identify topics that the tweet is about. This hashtag phrase counts against the 140 character limit though. Anyone can create or contribute to a hashtag, and it's here that many find another use for Twitter. Essentially, by using hashtags or searching for specific terms, you can instantly view everyone who is tweeting about a topic or an ongoing event, such as a presidential debate, sporting event or entertainment awards ceremony, and see what they have to say about it.

Hashtags are essentially Twitter's way to automatically provide a filtering and sorting mechanism for user updates. But you can also search for any words or phrases you want to see if anyone is tweeting about these topics. Note that Twitter is only able to search back a few days though, because of the sheer volume of posts that are occurring each day.

Because tweets can only be 140 characters in length, space is at a premium, so tweets make heavy use of link shortening websites, with Twitter even automatically shortening website links to make them take up as little space as possible. While this practice can be great for helping you pack information into your posts, it provides scammers with an easy way to persuade users to click on nefarious links, since Twitter users aren't as afraid of shortened, unrecognizable links (which may lead anywhere) as they are on other parts of the Internet.

LEARNING THE LINGO

Here are a few key Twitter terms defined, courtesy of the Twitter Glossary. You can visit the online dictionary for a full list of commonplace Twitter phrases.

@ – The @ sign is used to call out usernames in Tweets, like this: Hello @Twitter! When a username is preceded by the @ sign, it becomes a link to a Twitter profile. See also Replies and Mentions.

BLOCKING – To block someone on Twitter means they will be unable to follow you or add you to their lists, and the service will not deliver their mentions to your mentions tab.

DIRECT MESSAGE – Also called a DM and most recently called simply a "message," these Tweets are private between the sender and recipient. Tweets sent over texting services become DMs when they begin with "d username" to specify who the message is for.

FOLLOW – To follow someone on Twitter is to subscribe to their tweets or updates on the site.

FOLLOWER – A follower is another Twitter user who has followed you.

HASHTAG – The # symbol is used to mark keywords or topics in a Tweet. It was created organically by Twitter users.

MENTION – Mentioning another user in your tweet by including the @ sign followed directly by their username is called a "mention." This term also refers to tweets in which your username was included.

PROFILE – A Twitter page displaying information about a user, as well as all the Tweets they have posted from their account.

PROMOTED TWEETS – Tweets that selected businesses have paid to promote at the top of search results on Twitter.

PRIVATE ACCOUNTS – Also known as Protected Accounts. Twitter accounts are public by default. Choosing to protect your account means that your tweets will only be seen by approved followers and will not appear in search results.

RETWEET (noun) – A tweet by another user, forwarded to you by someone you follow. Often used to spread news or share valuable findings on Twitter.

RETWEET (verb) – To retweet, retweeting, retweeted. The act of forwarding another user's tweet to all of your followers.

RT – Abbreviated version of "retweet." Placed before the retweeted text when users manually retweet a message.

TRENDING TOPIC – A subject algorithmically determined to be one of the most popular on Twitter at the moment.

TWEET (verb) – Tweet, tweeting, tweeted. The act of posting a message, often called a "tweet," on Twitter.

TWEET (noun) – A message posted via Twitter containing 140 characters or fewer.

POTENTIAL ISSUES WITH TWITTER

Hacking – Hacking occurs when someone gains unauthorized access to an account and then posts unauthorized tweets or messages. If you use Twitter, be very suspicious of direct messages that ask you to click a link, especially from a person you don't know.

Impersonation – Impersonation is the practice of pretending to be someone else with the intention to deceive. This is different than parody accounts, which exist and are actually embraced by Twitter in which users pretend to be others for the sake of entertainment, and clearly state that they are not the real person being portrayed.

Phishing – Phishing is the practice of tricking a user in order to convince them give up their sensitive personal information. This can happen by sending the user links that go to a fake login page, or just simply asking for their username and password via a DM or email.

Spam – Unwanted messages or follows on Twitter. Twitter doesn't like the fact that there's Twitter spam any more than you do, and encourages you to report it.

If Facebook is the 800lb gorilla of the social media world, then Twitter is the 795lb one. Its influence can't be ignored, and its appeal to teens and tweens is that it allows for all the benefits of texting and more – and they can enjoy these upsides quickly, and without parents and grandparents following them.

Like Facebook and other popular social networks, Twitter is free to use, and has reached the point of critical mass – it's almost expected that kids will be connected to it in some form. The service is also becoming a de facto news source for the latest breaking events and happenings, and for discussing trending topics. It moves at lightning-fast pace, but a user's tweets can be easily viewed on their profile.

Because Twitter is very public in nature, and impulse-driven, there's always the chance that kids may do or say things they'll regret, since communications here are seemingly quick and disposable. Although there are blocking options and privacy features provided, for the most part anyone can follow anyone else, so it's easy to see how connections can be made with folks that kids may not want to be connected to as well. Still, it bears noting that Twitter is utilized by millions on a daily basis in perfectly positive, uplifting and rewarding manners – including as a means to share news, boost awareness for their community and connect and converse with like-minded individuals worldwide.

GOOGLE+

What It Is: Although it may lag behind the dominance and global popularity of Facebook, Google+ remains an important and influential social network simply based on the fact that it's from Google. When the company announced a suite of upgrades and design changes to the service in April 2012, it boasted 170 million accounts – not an inconsiderable amount by any estimation. That number has grown to more than 300 million accounts today.

Unsurprisingly, Google+ has had to carve out its own selling points and singular personality separate from those Facebook boasts in order to keep users coming back for more. Case in point: You can use Google+ to more effectively group contacts and start conversations with specific people using the concept of Circles, which is central to Google+. One of the key differences with this service as compared to other social networks isn't just its awesome Hangouts function which lets you chat with multiple parties in real-time. It's also how much emphasis is placed on keeping the public and private separate, and controlling whom you share information with.

On a happy note, Google+ seems to be here to stay. Google is diligently integrating the social network into other products such as YouTube, online search and Gmail, and it continues to grow in popularity with each passing month.

Who's On It: According to research reports, Google+ users are predominantly male, and the service is especially popular amongst web designers, engineers and students. However, many women and professionals from other backgrounds also use it as well. A useful place to conduct group conversations, or share links, articles and information with specific audiences as opposed to stream-of-consciousness-style status updates, it's increasingly becoming popular across the globe with all age groups.

Why Your Kids Will Want to Use It: In addition to focused sharing and communication via circles, teens will love video Hangouts' simple interface, which makes it easy to have a webcam conversation with multiple friends at the same time. Research shows that kids often use webcams like we as parents use phones, keeping them on and running while they are doing their homework or other activities, instead of simply being used during times of active engagement. Between the ability to casually videoconference with friends, and tightly manage information, it's easy to see the appeal for children – especially those with Android devices, or who prefer a more technically-inclined alternative to traditional social networks.

Ways to Connect: Circles lie at the heart of Google+, which revolves around various groups that you've setup to share different types of content with. Think of them as groups of people with common backgrounds or interests, i.e. coworkers, family members or individuals you know from after-school activities. Even though you may have given each of these Circles a name, these names are never visible to others, although the Circle itself and its members can be set to appear on your profile. Within each post you make on Google+, you can choose whom to make the shared information available to, whether it's visible to everyone, specific connections, or certain Circles. However, anyone who can view your posts can not only see all the comments made within the post, but can also share it with others.

Notable Points for Parents: In March of 2012, Google made waves by unfurling a unified privacy policy that essentially makes all the activity engaged in while signed into one's user account accessible to the company for the purposes of gathering information for advertising. But while all your usage data with regard to Google services is now governed by one umbrella privacy policy, the company does provide extensively customizable privacy settings in Google+, so there are the specific ways you can tweak your settings to enjoy more control over your information.

To access these settings, simply click on your name, and click on the link called "Privacy." Find the settings for Google+ and tweak these different settings. Google+ also has special features in place just for users between 13 and 18 years old. There are also pop-up warnings and restrictions encountered when communicating or sharing information with those outside of your preferred circles. Google+ also provides feature settings which allow you to choose which fields and information about you are searchable and that may appear in online search results. You can choose what information will be made available to specific individuals, circles and the world at large.

You can also control who you want to receive notifications from whenever someone shares a post with you, mentions you, invites you to a game or hangout, or shares a photo with you. You can keep this activity within your circle, or choose to allow either extended Circles or anyone to be able to include you in posts and send you these notifications. One setting you'll want to make sure to be aware of is which of your circles are included in the "Your Circles" settings. The service defaults to including everyone, but you can customize exactly who is included in the "Your Circles" sharing setting.

You can also tweak photo settings to control who can tag you and what information is provided in tags, and configure notifications to control whether or not you are notified when someone comments on a photo after you did or in a photo you were tagged in. One other privacy setting to be aware of with regard photos on Google+ involves the use of Google's facial recognition technology. Specifically, you have the choice as to whether to allow Google to try and recognize your face and prompt people you know to tag you.

As previously noted, Google+ also features what are called Hangouts, which are essentially webcam-based meetings in which multiple users can simultaneously appear on the same screen and videoconference. You'll need to be invited by someone that's in your circle to start a Hangout, or you can start your own. Other times, viewers can publicly tune in and watch others' video chats, which many celebrities and news organizations organize to discuss a relevant topic.

Each time you start or join a Hangout, you have the chance to check your appearance on-screen and adjust your microphone and speaker volume before you're visible to others. Make sure you're using common sense here, and if you're joining a Hangout that's not just with friends and family members, to hide any sensitive or potentially embarrassing items in background scenes, including not sharing anything that may inadvertently give away your personal data or address.

LEARNING THE LINGO:

There are a small list of key terms to note here compiled by the Google+ community. We've pulled a couple from there and added some of our own to give you a look at some of the primary turns of phrase associated with Google+ that all parents should know.

CIRCLE – The heart of Google+, this is how users organize their friends, groups and everyone they're following. After circles are defined, you decide which ones you want to share content or start a discussion with. Users can have multiple circles.

HANGOUT – Videoconferencing for up to ten attending through the browser using a webcam.

RIPPLES – The ripple diagram shows all public posts spreading as users share (Reshare) it on Google+. Arrows indicate the direction of resharing. via +Albert Albs

SHARED CIRCLE – When you create a circle of people on G+ and share it through your profile

STREAM – Real–time posts of people you follow, in chronological order, with the most recent on top.

Because of Google's broad reach and dominance in other areas like online search, email, maps and even Internet video viewing, Google+ offers plenty of easy integration options across a range of everyday services you and your kids likely already use. Although Circles may take a bit of time to set up and manage, they do provide a handy and elegant way to partition your contacts by interests and personal relation. More complex than other services, it's also less widely utilized – however, numbers continue to swell as time passes. Tech-savvy teens may feel more comfortable networking here than on Facebook on Twitter as parents are less likely to be active users.

PINTEREST

What It Is: Pinterest describes itself as "a virtual pinboard to organize and share the things you love" and it's one of the fastest-growing social networks today, quickly becoming the third-largest social network in the world less than two years after its launch in 2010. The site allows for "posting" of images along with a small description, capped at 500 words. These images can be from an article that you liked reading, a place you want to go on vacation, an item you want to buy — really, any photo you want to share on the web can be posted on Pinterest. You can choose to post these shots and visual montages to your own personal Pinterest boards, and you can maintain as many collages as you want.

If the concept still doesn't entirely make sense, think of it as a virtual scrapbook. Pinterest functions sort of like an inspiration board, or digital version of a real-life bulletin board, which may help the concept of "pinning" something up on your "board" seem more relatable. However, the boards we're discussing here live on your Pinterest profile, you can maintain as many as you want, and you can decide what to put on each one. Pinterest does offer some suggestions for posting when you first log on, but each board is fully customizable and can easily be changed to reflect personal tastes and interests.

Why Your Kids Will Want to Use It: Kids love using Pinterest because it's incredibly visual and easy to use, and functions like a virtual bulletin board online. Children can categorize their boards however they want, and share images and interests with others. Whether posting catalogue images, arts and crafts projects, vacation snapshots, or photos of cute boys, it's especially popular among teen girls.

Who's Using It: Pinterest exploded in popularity in 2011, driven heavily by female moms in the Midwest who used it to share recipes, home decorating ideas, teaching tips and more. As its user base has grown and expanded, it has become the go-to social network for anyone interested in specific topics or areas of interest to quickly find visual feedback.

Ways to Connect: Users can freely follow each other on Pinterest, usually finding each other because they are already connected on Facebook or other social networks. Following does not require mutual consent. You can choose to follow anyone you want on Pinterest, and they can choose to follow you, although there is a way to make your pinboards private.

When users log onto Pinterest, they can see a "stream" of pins from all the individuals that they follow and get caught up on the latest Pinterest ideas and whatnot. If they like what they see, they can easily repin the content, i.e. share it with others. Pinterest users can also seek out content to pin across the Web, and if a site doesn't have an automatic Pin button (similar to Twitter's tweet buttons and Facebook's share buttons), there's an easy way to select an image and post the web page to your Pinterest board.

Notable Points for Parents: Facebook, Twitter and Google+ are the names everyone knows about when it comes to social networking, but Pinterest has rapidly joined the short list of services that have gone mainstream. Teachers are using it as a great resource for planning lessons and connecting with students. Police departments are using it to spread positive messages to users within the community. Celebrities are using it, and even presidential candidates are getting on board (no pun intended), with both Michelle Obama and Ann Romney making frequent use of the service as part of the 2012 Presidential campaign.

PINTEREST ETIQUETTE

Pinterest itself suggests the following rules of etiquette, based on input from users.

Be Respectful – A great rule to remember on any social network, Pinterest also encourages users to respect one another despite differing tastes or opinions.

Be Authentic – Be who you are and embrace you are. For teens especially, this is an important message to promote, as many are struggling to find their identity and focus on interests they love. With Pinterest, they can easily find others who share the same passions or tastes.

Credit Your Sources – Although the core mechanic of Pinterest revolves around using others' content to spark conversation, Pinterest wants users to link to original sites, provide proper sourcing and not steal others' work.

Report Objectionable Content – As part of its Terms of Service, Pinterest does not allow the posting of nudity, hateful content or harmful material, and asks users to report any content which features any material that may be viewed as distasteful or inappropriate in nature.

POTENTIAL ISSUES WITH PINTEREST

With popularity on the Internet comes the risk of scammers and cybercriminals – naturally, these challenges present themselves on sites like Pinterest as well. Usually armed with the promise of items like a free gift card or giveaway, spammers attempt to get users to collect and click on links that can ask for personal information or spread malware. Be leery of any unknown links encountered on Pinterest just as you would anywhere else on the Internet and only click on them if you're 100% confident in where they'll take you.

Likewise, Pinterest blocks pornography and other unsavory material, but it's still possible to find boards that contain questionable content. Be aware that kids may come across inappropriate postings, and make sure they know how to react when these items are encountered. With the rise of smartphones and tablets, there are also a number of fake Pinterest apps that attempt to generate ad revenue or monitor the activity of users who download them thinking they are getting an official Pinterest product. Keep your eyes open and be aware of the potential risks.

PINTEREST SAFETY TIPS

Please follow these guidelines, offered courtesy of McAfee, to stay safe when using the popular social networking service:

• Never share your password with anyone. Such tools make it very easy to mass-comment or post from any account.

• If any web page asks you to "Pin It" before you can see the content, most likely it is a scam.

• If any web page offers you a "free gift card" and redirects you to surveys, most likely it is a scam.

• Be careful while clicking links that have catchy titles like "shocking video," "you will not believe it," "free giveaway," etc. Most of the time, they lead to scams and trouble!

SOURCE:
http://blogs.mcafee.com/mcafee-labs/peering-into-a-pinterest-scam-toolkit

LEARNING THE LINGO:

Pinterest is actually pretty intuitive once you get started, and with fairly straightforward functionality, there are only a few terms you need to know before you'll have master the service.

PINS – The main form of content of Pinterest. Each Pin consists of an image, a text description and usually a link. Users have the option to edit and create their own text for every pin they make.

PIN IT BUTTON – A free add-on for your Web browser or smartphone that allows you to easily identify and pin content to your pinboards while you're browsing the web at large. If you're on a page you want to share, you simply click the Pin It Button and you're able to choose an image and type a description and have the content sent to Pinterest, without ever leaving the page you're on.

BOARDS – Boards are the way that Pins are organized by users into larger groupings. Pinterest offers some generic ones to get you started, but you can edit and create your own, based on virtually any theme. For example, many women who are about to get married create boards for their weddings or showers. Moms like to pin ideas for birthday parties or arts and crafts projects. Some men even like to create Star Wars or beer-themed Boards. Each can be followed by the general public, unless it's made private.

REPINS — When a user re-shares a pin that they like, placing it on their own board, that's called a Repin. The act of repinning functions a bit like "retweets" on Twitter and "shares" on Facebook. When you repin something, you'll have a chance to tweak the text when posting, but it's not a necessity. But all content will ultimately look like it's coming from you.

LIKES — If you like a pin, but not enough to repin it, you can still like it as way to show support and encouragement. Pinterest also keeps a board for everything a user likes, and you or others can quickly view all the pins you've liked.

SNAPCHAT

What It Is: Snapchat is a video messaging application created by Evan Spiegel, Bobby Murphy, and Reggie Brown, then Stanford University students, and it was launched in 2011. Using the application, users can take photos, record videos, add text and drawings, and send them to a controlled list of recipients. Today, more than 700 million photos are shared using this mobile app every day.

What's really interesting about Snapchat is users send these photos and videos to recipients to be viewed only for a pre-determined amount of time, from one to ten seconds, after which they will be hidden form the recipient's device but not deleted from Snapchat's servers.

What's also interesting is in 2013, Snapchat created SnapKidz, which is like Snapchat, except the kids who register to use it can't share images or videos. Instead, they are only allowed to take snaps, draw on them and then save those images locally on their device.

Why Your Kids Will Want to Use It: Kids love using Snapchat because it's a fun way for them to share their on-going life experiences with friends, a sort of visual conversation, if you will. Snapchat allows kids to share a photo of the meal they're about to eat, a wacky expression they're making, a funny thing they spotted on the way to school. It's a way to share moments with friends without making them permanent. The motivation for creating the service, Spiegel said, was to create something that provided more privacy than Facebook and other social networks.

But just because the images are deleted doesn't mean that they can't be captured. In fact, some smartphones allow recipients to capture the screens. Others, including a dad who was concerned about his daughter's experience being cyberbullied, have found ways to capture the images shared on this service using another cell phone camera. Still others who are security experts have used their forensic computing skills to expose deleted photos.

Who's Using It: Since its debut in 2011, Snapchat has exploded in popularity, and today, users are sharing more than 700 million photos and videos each day.

Ways to Connect: Users send snaps to a designated person or group of people. After reading or viewing the snap, the snap disappears in ten seconds. Viewers can respond to the snaps with snaps or commentary on their own. It's a way to hold visual and video conversations. By drawing on photos or videos and adding their own spin on things, it's also a way to be creative.

Notable Points for Parents: Snapchat is not meant for anyone younger than 13. SnapKidz is a version younger children can register for – and at the time of registration, kids are required to input their ages, and unlike Snapcat, SnapKidz doesn't let children send images. But savvy kids will save the snaps and upload them using other apps.

POTENTIAL ISSUES WITH SNAPCHAT

Sharing images and videos that disappear after viewing creates a different subset of issues than other social networks like Facebook or Twitter, where the images and comments live on. One issue is that the very spontaneity that this type of interaction offers could encourage some children to be rude or to bully others. An example of bullying, as a father responded to it on YouTube, can be found here:

www.myfoxtwincities.com/story/2789782 9/prior-lake-dad-turns-to-youtube-to-rep ort-snapchat-bully.

One important preventive to bullying is to make sure your child manages his or her settings appropriately. If you don't want your child receiving snaps from just anybody, make sure you set your default setting to only accept incoming media from "My Friends" on Snapchat. For more information on setting these features up correctly, visit:

support.snapchat.com/a/privacy-settings

To prevent some instances of bullying, make sure your children only share snaps with friends, and make sure they know how to send snaps and how to block snaps. Here's a link to learn how to block senders whom you no longer wish to receive snaps from:

https://support.snapchat.com/a/block-frie nds.

If inappropriate messages of any nature are sent or received, you can also report abuse at: https://support.snapchat.com/ca/abuse-other or email Snapchat at safety@snapchat.com.

One of the biggest concerns parents have about Snapchat is its potential for sexting and the sending and receiving of inappropriate images. Recent studies have shown that the amount of sexting in general is way, way less than what parents think it is. According to a study by the Pediatrics medical journal, at least seven percent of teens sent or received nude or partially nude images.

If your child sends or receives inappropriate images, you can always delete the account by going to https://accounts.snapchat.com/accounts/ delete_account as long as you have the username and password. If you don't have the name or password, you can submit a request for deletion at: https://www.snapchat.com/static_files/deletion_request.pdf.

Lastly, although snaps are, by their nature, designed to be as fleeting as a moment in regular life, users have found ways to save snaps and upload them to more permanent forms of social media. Your children should be advised that while Snapchat was designed to be spontaneous, people can still find ways to get around supposed limitations.

LEARNING THE LINGO:

SNAPS – The main form of content of Snapchat. Each snap consists of a photo or image, and users can decide whether they disappear in one to ten seconds after they're initially viewed..

STORIES – If you want to share more than a single moment, you can string several of them together to create stories, and stories stick around for 24 hours.

CHATS – Instead of sharing snaps with all of your friends, you can enjoy one-on-one chats with individual friends. Like regular snaps, chats usually disappear quickly, as once both parties leave the chat, the messages disappear, but messages can be saved by either person, and when they are saved, they are saved on both screens.

SNAPCASH – This feature isn't allowed for users under 18, but some children and teens do take advantage of parents' debit cards to pay someone back via Snapchat. Adult users of Snapchat can link their Snapchat and debit card accounts to make "peer to peer" payments.

INSTAGRAM

What It Is: Instagram is a photo-sharing, video-sharing and social networking service that enables its users to take pictures and videos and share them on other social networking platforms like Facebook and Twitter. It was created by Kevin Systrom and Mike Krieger in 2010, and as it rose in popularity, Facebook purchased it for $1 billion in 2012. It's an especially popular platform for sharing images, photos and other forms of visual communications.

Why Your Kids Will Want to Use It: Kids love using Instagram because it's one of the easiest ways to capture and then share photos and videos. Why write a post or respond to the question of "what are you doing" with another post when you can simply share a video or photo? Kids love taking, cropping, enhancing, and sharing images, as well as liking photos and commenting on photos. Instagram is a mixed media conversation, and it's a place where teens love to talk.

Who's Using It: Instagram has exploded in popularity since its founding, with more than 300 million active users and more than 30 billion photos shared.

Ways to Connect: Instagram allows teens to take, crop, share and comment on photos and videos, and it allows users to edit and enhance these forms of multimedia, allowing a personal sense of style and creativity to emerge. Because teens can like and comment on photos and links, it also allows teens to connect and socialize in a environment rich with visual imagery.

Notable Points for Parents: Like many social networks, those under 13 aren't allowed to join the conversation on Instagram, and Instagram will remove underage users if alerted. That said, lots of younger kids use Instagram, just as lots of younger kids use Facebook.

One of the main challenges for parents is to teach teens how photos – photos they take, which are tagged on and are posted – can reflect an image of who they are to the world, and that this image is going to be seen by teachers, potential employers and college admissions professionals. It might seem obvious, but any content and photos posted online are pretty difficult, even nearly impossible, to take back.

It is important for teens to know how they can hide photos from their profiles and untag themselves – i.e. make these images still visible but not linked back to their usernames and profiles. It's also important for them to know that if they don't want photos of themselves to automatically be added to the section called "Photos of You," they can do so simply by turning off the "Add Automatically" feature.

While the actual content of photos needs to be considered by teens as well, they also need to be instructed to look at the background of the photos. A photo of a teen at a party where a keg appears in the background might be a definite turn-off to potential employers, for example.

Another aspect of Instagram that parents need to consider is whether to keep their teens' profiles private. For many who use Instagram, part of the fun is developing a big following. Whether you want this for your children or not is something to discuss. Having a private account means that your teen has to approve anyone who wants to follow him or her, but just having a private account does not mean that your teen will automatically not be shown in photos posted elsewhere or on other sites because teens like to take photos of each other.

POTENTIAL ISSUES WITH INSTAGRAM

The main challenge of Instagram – and the sharing of any photos and videos online anywhere – is managing one's image, and that's something that teens particularly, who are caught in the moment of sharing a silly or funny photo, might not recognize as important.

As mentioned in the previous section, one of the most important things tweens and teens can learn about Instagram is how they untag themselves. Sometimes,

a teen might encounter someone who harasses them, or repeatedly tags them in photos they dislike, sending them a lot of uncomfortable messages. Teens need to know that they can block these users so they can't tag them, contact them directly or even mention them in comments. Under Instagram's basic menu, there's a feature called "Block User."

Kids can also delete videos and photos they've posted. That doesn't mean that these videos are gone forever – someone else could have copied them and posted them elsewhere – but that deletes them directly from Instagram.

As with Facebook and Twitter, Instagram allows users to report inappropriate photos, videos and comments, as well as anyone who violates Instagram's community guidelines.

LEARNING THE LINGO:

LIKE – Just "like" Facebook, you can "like" photos, videos, and comments, and it simply shows as a thumbs up.

COMMENT – A comment is just that – a comment on a photo or video, and it is shared with other users.

STREAM – Your stream reveals all the photos and videos of people you follow.

#HASHTAG – #Hashtags allow you to search for photos and videos of things and people you want to follow.

COLLAGE – Many people post collages of sets of photos that they take and then post on Instagram. Collage is actually not a feature of Instagram, but another app called Diptic allows you to create the collage and then post it on Instagram.

VIRTUAL WORLDS AND ONLINE GAMES

What They Are: In a quest to become the main destination for kids online, companies large and small oftentimes create virtual online worlds for kids. Dedicated Internet spaces where kids can connect, communicate and/or play games while hanging out with friends, all invite users to spend time in each others' company and share in activities. Sounds a bit like social networks, no? In essence, that's what these services are, although often times with more emphasis on flashy graphics and fun time-killing exploits.

Although most can be accessed by simply typing the right URL into your web browser, some may require software downloads, or that you purchase a disc at a local retail outlet. In any given case, as you and your kids will soon discover, despite the "free" tag many boast, not everything provided in these worlds is truly free. In fact, many online worlds have recently moved from a onetime purchase price and/or subscription-based business model to "freemium" or free-to-play solutions. In essence, anyone can access these games or certain slices of them at no cost, but in order to enjoy access to added features, or more areas, items and fun stuff within their confines, kids need to make one-off purchases, or pay a monthly or even annual subscription fee.

Major corporations spend ample effort to attract players to virtual worlds, because it not only provides a healthy source of income, it also offers a way for them to market themselves and expose their brand to youngsters on a regular basis, all while staying compliant with laws about privacy and data collection. Many household names such as McDonald's, Disney and General Mills provide online spaces for kids to spend time in, although a few have recently come under fire for their use of a "refer-a-friend" features, which many advocacy groups say are in violation of COPPA laws.

Several of these virtual worlds are aimed at tweens and teens. Games like Wizard 101, FreeRealms, Minecraft and Lord of the Rings Online all strive to be a place where older elementary-aged kids spend their time online, as well as their money. Other virtual worlds are aimed squarely at younger Internet users. Club Penguin, Animal Jam, Jump Start, Starfall and even Build-A-Bear Workshop are all examples of persistent online destinations created to attract young tots, and many tout their educational benefits.

Naturally, there are others that hope to fill in the gaps between these groups. Little Space Heroes, Fantage, Fusion Fall and Moshi Monsters all blend elements of traditional video games with the easy access of browser-based online games.

There are even virtual worlds for families, which allow for loved ones and friends scattered around the globe to connect and play games with each other asynchronously.

The concept of online virtual worlds makes a lot of sense from the perspective of developers, and the proposition can be appealing for parents as well. Instead of simply setting kids free in the Internet's vast and unregulated spaces, virtual worlds provide a means by which kids can spend large chunks of time in one safe environment, where they can find games, activities and chances to interact with others. That peace of mind is even worth a considerable sum each month for some parents.

Why Your Kids Will Want To Use Them: There are a number of reasons why kids love spending time in these worlds, from feeling like they're having their own space to engage in to being able to interact with friends and go on adventures in a fun, mutually-shared environment. And here's where we start to get to some of the potential danger areas. One of the key features of these virtual worlds is that they allow some sort of contact with others, even if it's just in the ability to compare scores. Most virtual worlds do include the option to chat or communicate with others, and it's here that the proposition of virtual worlds can start to get dicey for many. While many include some form of moderated or restricted communications, nearly all provide some way to access (with parental permission) the ability to chat with strangers.

Who's Using Them: There are virtual worlds designed for nearly every age, from Jumpstart for Preschoolers and Club Penguin for early elementary aged kids to World of Warcraft, whose fans range from teenagers to baby boomers. Although some virtual worlds can appeal to a specific set and others to a broad range of ages, nearly every kid who spends time online has probably seen some sort of invitation to join one. According to research firm KZero, even several years ago, there were nearly 1.2 billion registered users across all virtual worlds, the largest group being kids aged 10-15.

Ways to Connect: Most of these virtual worlds are free to access, just like the rest of the Internet. Getting there is as simple as typing the correct address in your web browser, and all of a sudden you're transported to a medieval land, outer space, or even an island inspired by a fast food restaurant. However, some virtual worlds – especially those aimed at older kids – can require separate software downloads and installations to play, and function more like traditional video games, though they're often still free to play, at least at first.

Notable Points for Parents: While online virtual worlds are an incredibly popular way to have fun with friends on the Internet in a seemingly trustworthy environment, the truth is that there are a number of potential concerns and dangers that parents and users of all ages should be aware of. The European Network and Information Security Agency (ENISA) reports that the biggest concerns for parents about virtual worlds for both kids (7 and under) and tweens (8 to 12) is online safety and exposure to online predators. This is made possible due to the very social nature of these virtual worlds, which are essentially forms of social networks for kids with more of an emphasis on graphics than words.

Going beyond general online safety fears, key concerns parents have about virtual worlds according to the ENISA include:

• Exposure to harmful or illegal content, such as pornography or gambling
• Interaction with ill-intentioned adults masquerading as children
• Identity theft
• Health issues related to spending too much time on the computer and not enough time outside
• Unauthorized spending

While these are all legitimate concerns, all reputable virtual world sites take steps to prevent misuse or abuse by users which parents should be aware of. For starters, any service aimed at kids age 13 and under must be compliant with the U.S.'s stringent COPPA regulations, designed to protect the online privacy of minors. The creators of sites that are used by kids also frequently offer many privacy and regulation options via parental controls settings, which can also sometimes generate usage reports illustrating not only how long kids tend to play, but what types of activities they've been participating in.

And because gamers in these virtual worlds are always connected online, the game's developers can track and record every movement, interaction and purchase that gamers make while online. Companies do this not necessarily with the player's best interests in mind, but rather to be able to better tune and enhance their worlds based on how players are using them. However, for parents concerned about online safety, this practice proves a handy coincidence. Note that for those parents worried about maintaining their children's privacy, at least some degree of anonymity will usually be sacrificed by participating in virtual worlds, even if the data collected can't be connected to your kids, specifically.

MANAGING ONLINE CHAT FUNCTIONS

Community is frequently a large part of virtual worlds' appeal, with social interaction often a main reason for engaging with these products – a key part of these products is therefore the chat function. Happily, there are many solutions available to help prevent unwanted and undesired contact from others.

There are two ways that chat can be moderated in virtual worlds. The first is by controlling which other users players can interact with (i.e. simply managing friends lists), and the second involves determining which types of communication they can engage in.

As a basic option, many virtual worlds offer "restricted chat" features. Using such options not only restricts users to talking only with others on approved friends list, but often also limits exchanges to default, pre-provided chat options participants can select and use. Older kids may be allowed more freedom to converse, but it's worth nothing that most virtual worlds still have a list of words they will not allow and filter out profanity automatically, though users may use slang or shorthand to try and circumvent these restrictions.

In any circumstance, nearly all services offer live, human moderators that are on hand and roaming worlds with an eye towards looking for any bad or questionable behavior. Even when you cannot find administrators who are in-character, virtually every service offers access to support staff who can immediately respond should you click a handy and usually prominent "report" button, or reach out via similar channels for help.

KEEPING KIDS SAFE IN VIRTUAL WORLDS

The US government provides a website at OnGuardOnline.gov that offers many online safety tips, including those specific to online games and virtual worlds. Among the recommendations provided is that parents check out online destinations themselves and engage in specific conversations about how and when they'll be visiting these virtual worlds to check up on children. Parents can also look for third-party certifications on these sites such as the TRUSTe online privacy Trustmark, the kidSAFE Seal or the FamilyFriendlyVideoGames.com Seal of Approval. All indicate that the site has been checked out by a third-party to ensure it's a trusted solution that takes pains to address children's safety, privacy and other concerns.

LEARNING THE LINGO

To make sure parents and interested parties have a solid understanding of how virtual worlds operate, following is a look at 10 of the most important phrases associated with them:

AVATARS: Avatars are the 2D or 3D virtual representation of your character that appears on-screen, and are often highly customizable by players. Usually, when you start out in a virtual world, you can tweak many of the basics of your character or profile photo's appearance, but as you play more, you'll earn special items and upgrades that can also be used to enhance or change your avatar's look and feel.

BETA: This is a term used by video game developers to indicate that a product is not quite final yet and is still in the testing phases. Such products may, however, still be accessible to the public, with an eye towards tweaking and testing as feedback is gained from public use of the product. The beta phase of a virtual world usually means much tinkering is going on behind the scenes as developers work to enhance and improve the title, and drastic changes may still be made to later editions based on observation, feedback and testing.

CHAT: A key feature in online virtual worlds, chat and messaging options are one of the more obvious ways that users occupying the same online space can communicate one another. Any reputable online virtual world will offer safeguards such as pre-scripted chat responses, safe chat features, the ability to approve or block specific users, blacklisting and filtering of prohibited words or phrases, as well as options to restrict whom others can chat with.

CURRENCY: Most online virtual worlds offer some sort of in-game currency which allows users to buy items or

upgrades for their dwelling or avatar. Whether referring to Rox in Moshi Monsters, Taro in FusionFall or simply Coins as commonly found in a number of other products, said currency effectively functions as in-game cash that can be spent on power-ups, equipment, and other goodies. This currency is frequently earned not only by playing games and collecting items inside the virtual world, but often is provided as a reward for logging in daily or playing bonus mini-games.

EMOTE: Emotes are character expressions that players can use to communicate with others in the game world without chatting, such as when avatars smile, shrug or frown. In essence, they're short animations that you can make your virtual alter-ego perform. Common examples include happy dances, laughs and fist-pumping cheers, and all can be prompted by a simple button press. Emotes let players either act silly or express themselves via virtual bodylanguage without needing to chat or engage in vocal communication.

FRIENDS: Friends in online games and virtual worlds are generally different than friends in real-life – the term typically refers to contacts and connections you've made, much as it does on other forms of social network. For younger kids, it's recommended that you keep friend relationships restricted to individuals they already know in real-life, and older kids may actually derive more enjoyment from online experiences if enjoying them alongside schoolyard pals. However, meeting new people, interacting with them, and going on adventures is a big part of virtual worlds' draw, and can be a perfectly safe and fun way for players to enjoy themselves. Note that friends in virtual worlds are usually connected only upon mutual acceptance, although characters can frequently send friend requests to any other avatar they come across in hopes of expanding their connections. Again, just because you're friends in a virtual world doesn't mean you've ever met in real life.

MEMBERSHIP: Although many virtual worlds offer at least some basic, enjoyable free-to-play experience, nearly all offer premium membership or subscription options which provide, for an additional monthly or yearly subscription fee, access to extra areas, games, items and adventures within the title. If your kids dabble in virtual worlds, be prepared for their inevitable pleas for membership, which can run anywhere from around $5 per month to more than $75 per year. Another term to note here as well are microtransactions – in-game purchases (typically $1-$20 in nature) that can be made on-demand, and provide more virtual currency, new items or other perks. All cost real-world cash to enjoy.

MODERATORS: Moderators are humans that participate and monitor virtual worlds and behavior within them in order to not only assist users who need help, but also to deal with any instances of cheating, misuse or players that are exhibiting negative or troubling behavior. Moderators may be secretly roaming the world as a player character, or be actively monitoring help lines should queries come through, issues be raised, or inappropriate activities be flagged by the system or by users for investigation.

REPORTING: Although moderators may be available to connect with, it's important for players to realize the power that they have to report questionable conduct, cheating or other in-game issues to the game's developers. Although it's easy to block other users and then report their behavior, players are also encouraged to report any problems or glitches they see in the game so the developers can fix them. This is especially true of titles that are in beta or early-release versions (e.g. alpha or prototype).

SERVERS: Setting aside the technical meaning of this term, which refers to remotely-located computer systems which power the online universe, from the user's standpoint, each server essentially represents a separate instance of a game or virtual world with its own landscape, characters and activity. Some of the more popular online games and worlds will have multiple server options available to help maximize speed and performance or provide variety in visuals or gameplay, with each server representing a parallel universe. It's important to note the name of the server you're playing on, especially if you are trying to meet any of your friends online. If you choose to play on different servers, you typically won't be able to play together in the same spaces of the virtual world.

With a basic understanding of the key concepts, concerns and terms to consider surrounding virtual worlds and online games under your belt, you're likely ready for some specific recommendations as to which you and your kids will want to enjoy. Next up is a look at some of the top high-tech picks to choose from.

VIRTUAL WORLDS FOR KIDS

We've given you the basic facts about virtual worlds, talked about some of the top concerns surrounding them, and broken down the 10 most important terms to know about these products. Now it's time to consider some leading recommendations. Following, you'll find a sample of several of the most popular online virtual worlds for kids. A few are personal favorites, and a few we had no choice but to include based on their popularity.

Animal Jam – Brought to you by National Geographic Kids, Animal Jam is aimed at elementary school-aged users and has an educational aspect to its minigames

and social interactions. Featuring cute, customizable animal characters, and events and happenings that change with the calendar, the title encourages players to come back again and again to experience different aspects of the game.

Club Penguin – Disney's most popular online world, Club Penguin is a wintry-themed collection of mini-games for players that are designed to be fun and highly replayable. Featuring appealing cartoon artwork and a quirky sense of humor, Club Penguin is designed for kids of all ages to enjoy, including very young children. There are extensive moderated chat and friend-filtering options available, and due to the size of the game's subscriber base, there are often many in-game charity drives that take place.

Fantage – Fantage is a virtual world for kids which provides customizable, cartoonish avatars that can be used to participate in a variety of fun and educational activities. Some of the games contained within it are designed to be enjoyed by multiple players, so enlisting your friend's help is encouraged. Many schools around the country even use Fantage's geography, logic and math games to enhance their curriculum.

FusionFall – FusionFall features characters and locations made famous by Cartoon Network's colorful cast.

Throughout the game, you'll meet grown-up and pint-sized versions of Ben 10, Dexter, the Powerpuff Girls, and more of the TV channel's top stars.

Little Space Heroes – Designed by parents, Little Space Heroes is built to be extremely kid- and family-friendly, placing players in the role of adorably customizable space heroes who travel to various themed planets such as a forest world or wintry wonderland. There, they'll take part in mini-games, solve mysteries and discover rare items. Memberships provide enhanced features and access to additional items, and are offered on a monthly and annual basis.

Minecraft – Minecraft is the ultimate online sandbox, in which players can create their own 3D structures and communities out of various types of bricks and objects, all while working to avoid attacks by monsters. The simplicity of the game's interface and objectives leads to tremendous depth and diversity both in terms of user-generated creations and play styles. There's a free sample version available on the site, or players can join the Minecraft world for a one-time fee.

Moshi Monsters – Moshi Monsters invites players to adopt an exceptionally cute pet monster, who must be lavished with a combination of funny, gross and weird items to be kept happy. Players will rely heavily on the game's in-game currency of Rox, playing daily mini-games to earn more money while connecting with friends. Moshi Monsters saw its popularity surge when it switched to a free-to-play model, and offers greatly enhanced memberships after players have already started which can be had on a monthly or annual basis.

Skylanders – This online virtual world serves as a companion to the wildly popular Skylanders video game franchise in which players use real-life figurine toys and place them on a "portal of power" to bring them to life within the game itself. Skylanders features the same art style, music and other sounds as may be found in other editions of the game, but is mostly a fun place to hang out and play with your creatures in different ways. The game is free-to-play, provided you have purchased Skylanders toys, which can be input into the game using either a USB-attached Portal of Power or the unique ID code that comes in every package.

Wizard 101 – Become a student at the Ravenwood School of Magical Arts and learn the various aspects of magic as you equip yourself for a battle against the evil Malistaire and his evil minions. Featuring elements of collection, combat and adventuring, Wizard 101 remains one of the most popular online virtual worlds with tens of millions of fans, and offers memberships starting at a reasonable monthly fee.

OTHER POPULAR VIRTUAL WORLDS:

- Babble Planet
- Barbie Girls
- Bearville
- Bella Sara
- Bin Weevils
- Build A Bearville
- Chobots
  Clone Wars Adventures
- Dinokids
- Dizzywood
- Franktown Rocks
- Freerealms
- Habbo
- Happy Meal
- Jumpstart
- MinyanLand
- Monkey Quest
- Neopets
- Pandanda
- Pirate 101
- Pirates of the Caribbean
- Pixie Hollow
- Planet Cazmo
- Poptropica
- PoraOra
- Secret Builders
- Stardoll
- Toontown Online
- Travels of Wiglington & Wenks
- Ty Girlz
- Webkinz
- Webosaurs
- Whyville

OTHER SOCIAL NETWORKS OF INTEREST

Here's a quick look at a few more social networks that may be of interest for kids. Consider the following not recommendations or endorsements, but rather a quick overview should you or your children be interested in learning more about these alternatives to more widely-known services. Note that services and features are constantly changing — you may find this list changes considerably over time.

Ban.Jo — Location-based service that aggregates other social network feeds to show where your friends are and what they're doing on a map-based interface.

Foursquare — This location-based website encourages users to check into locations to see who else is there, and provides rewards for specific or frequent check-ins.

Habbo — An online "virtual hotel" aimed at teens that is staffed by adult moderators, where kids take on the role of a character and use credits to participate in events or decorate their rooms while engaging and interacting with others.

Hachi — Aimed at jobseekers and corporate clients, Hachi provides a ready way to find networking connections within specific industries or areas of business.

Highlight — An iPhone app that connects you with other users that have the app that are in close proximity. You'll get notifications when friends are close by, and even introductions and information when strangers with the app are near, too.

Instagram — Photo-sharing social network which lets users follow one another and discover other pictures they like, and makes it possible to easily share images with other social networks. Purchased by Facebook in 2012.

Kismet — Location-based app that uses social media profiles to maintain an updated identity which is then broadcast and shared with other Kismet users nearby. It is now part of Yahoo!

LinkedIn — Useful for anyone in or entering the job market, LinkedIn helps make connections on a professional level, and has a robust selection of groups where users can share common expertise.

Nextdoor — Designed to be used locally as a private social network for your neighborhood, Nextdoor allows you to meet neighbors, discuss issues of shared interest, and ultimately keep the neighborhood safer through ongoing communications.

Path – Bills itself as a personal journal of your life that is only shared with family and close friends, so you can pass along messages, updates and announcements to those you love and trust most.

Quora – A question and answer site wherein users can put questions to the public, answer others' queries and even promotethe responses they like the most.

Reddit – A user-generated news service in which users post links to stories that they find interesting, which other users can vote on to provide added support and visibility. The social networking aspect of this service involves commenting, sharing and voting on said stories.

So.Cl – Invites users to connect around specific topics, with easy chat and video chat options embedded in its interface.

StumbleUpon – Offers a way for users to discover new and interesting content by exploring areas they are already interested in and receiving recommendations based on their tastes.

Tagged – Tagged bills itself "The Social Network for Meeting New People" and seeks to connect users with other like-minded fans, whether to try and start a relationship or just play games together.

Tumblr–A short-form blogging platform that allows for quick updates and photo sharing, and lets users easily follow each other or discover other content that may be of interest.

Yik Yak – This app is targeted more towards adults, especially college students, as it is an anonymous social media app that allows users to anonymously create and view news and gossip or "yaks" within a 10-mile radius. Users can contribute to the content by writing, responding and up- or down-voting "yaks."

YouTube – Although you may not think of the world's most popular video aggregator as a social network, there are a number of features which make YouTube an online community, such as the ability to comment on others' videos, like clips, and follow specific users or companies with dedicated YouTube channels.

CONCLUSION

While many are quick to decry the widespread acceptance of social networks as emblematic of current and future societal problems involving kids' use of technology, these services remain some of the most popular, interesting and informative destinations on the Web today. Moreover, they're sure to play a prominent and ongoing role in 21st century life, making them impossible to ignore or dismiss outright.

On the bright side, there are a number of positive aspects to social networks which we're only beginning to understand and explore, such as their ability to promote philanthropy or social activism and even provide potential psychological and health-related benefits, including their potential to provide positive support and affirmation for those who need it most. However, there are also concerns associated with social networks which we as a society have yet to fully comprehend, such as the long-term ramifications and effects of constantly-connected Internet activity, and what effect it has on developing minds.

Ongoing debate and dialogue about social networks and their impact on today's generations is vital to staying ahead of the curve. As modern parents and educators, it's important to constantly be seeking out new information, researching emerging tools and trends, and engaging in conversation with experts, thought leaders and the broader community about these emerging topics. Taking the time to read this work underscores your commitment to learning, growth and development, and helping educate and inform Generation Tech about the technology which promises to shape its life going forward – an effort which we applaud. But it's merely the first step in an ongoing lifelong journey for kids and adults alike.

We urge you to consistently be seeking out more information, going hands-on with new features and services, and connecting with other parents, teachers, law enforcement officials, and families about the issues and concerns surrounding social networks. Only by doing so can we hope to stay adequately equipped and informed, and thereby keep our families safe for years to come.

While the digital footprints that are being defined now may not persist for thousands of years as pre-historic cave paintings have done, they are important to note. The images currently being painted by and about us online on the walls of today's social networks promise to linger for decades to come, and have a profound effect on both the way our lives progress and broader world at large. Moreover, all can serve to help forge meaningful connections across vast distances and ages – if we use them wisely, positively, and for the greater good. We sincerely hope that you and your family will continue to utilize social networks, enjoy them safely and responsibility, and take part in this ongoing voyage of discovery. It's one which – when the path of understanding, empathy and awareness is followed – only promises to make social networks a brighter and more uplifting part of the world for tomorrow's family.

ADDITIONAL RESOURCES

Children's Online Safety – The California Department of Department of Justice, Office of the Attorney General has a whole section of its website dedicated to protecting children online. The site features resources and educational programs for parents and educators.

Common Sense – Digital Literacy Curriculum – Common Sense Media offers ratings on many popular products, and a free Digital Literacy and Citizenship Curriculum to help educators empower students and school communities to be safe, responsible, and savvy as they navigate the fast-paced digital world.

Common Sense Media – Resources for Educators – Features programs for educators and students, and professional development tools to help with all aspects of online education for kids.

Connect Safely Guide To Facebook – This 36-page guide dedicated exclusively to Facebook safety for families isprovided courtesy of Internet Safety experts Larry Magid and Anne Collier.

ConnectSafely's Comprehensive Guide to Online Safety Resources – A thorough list of resources from across the Web dealing with many aspects of online safety.

CyberCitizen Awareness Program – The Cybercitizen Awareness Program educates children and young adults on the dangers and consequences of cybercrime. By reaching out to parents and teachers, the program is designed to establish a broad sense of responsibility and community in an effort to develop smart, ethical and socially conscious online behavior in young people.

CyberCrime.gov – The Computer Crime and Intellectual Property Section (CCIPS) is responsible for implementing the Department of Justice's national strategies for combating computer and intellectual property crimes worldwide.

CyberSmart! – CyberSmart! fosters 21st century skills that increase student engagement and prepare pupils to achieve in today's digital society.

CyberTipLine – The Congressionally–mandated CyberTipline is a means for reporting crimes against children. Think of it as "911"emergency services for the Internet.

DigitalCitizenship.net – An overview and summary of coreonline citizenship concepts, with links to resources and descriptions of the nineelements of digital citizenship.

Digizen – The Digizen website provides useful information on appropriate online use for educators, parents, caretakers, and young people. It's designed to be used to strengthen their awareness and understanding of what digital citizenship is and encourages users of technology to be and become responsible digital citizens.

Facebook Family Safety Center – Facebook safety page featuring broad overviews of key issues to be concerned with and how to combat them as well as detailed information for teachers, teens, parents and law enforcement officials.

FTC – COPPA Explanation – A guide from the FTC that answers frequently asked questions about the Children's Online Privacy Protection Act (COPPA).

GetNetWise.org – GetNetWise aims to help ensure that Internet users have safe, constructive, and educational or entertaining online experiences by offering links to resources and information about a number of online issues.

Google Family Safety Channel – Offers a series of videos from Google that illustrate how to keep kids safe online.

kidSAFE Seal –The kidSAFE® Seal Program is a "seal of approval" program that independently reviews and certifies the safety practices of child-friendly websites and applications, including kid-targeted video game sites, virtual worlds, social networks, mobile apps, web-connected devices, and other similar Interactive products.

McAfee Security Advice Center – Provides hints, tips and advice on issues such as identity theft protection and Internet security.

NetSmartz – A resource provided by the National Center for Missing & Exploited Children that's designed to help inform and educate parents who may not be familiar with the technology and online services that kids are using.

Professor Garfield – Offers a series of videos starring popular cartoon character Garfield and friends about issues such as Cyberbullying and Online Safety.

Social Safety – SocialSafety.org is a public service that was created to provide information and resources to help families stay safe while participating in an online community of friends.

StaySafeOnline.org – Offers hints, tips and actionable curriculums for families, teachers and businesses looking to learn more about online safety.

Symantec Online Family Safety Guide – Features insights into a variety of online safety issues for children and teens from Internet security experts.

That Girl in Pink – That Girl in Pink Foundation is a nonprofit organization dedicated to the prevention of teen suicide.The foundation was formed specifically to provide support, advice, and education to teenagers on issues that relate to them and help them cope with the challenges they face growing up in a connected world.

Trend Micro Internet Safety and Security – Provides resources, topics and a must-see yearly video contest designed to help teens spread the message to their peers about key online safety issues.

Twitter Safety Tips for Parents – A page designed for parents to answer questions about key aspects of teen safety for users of the popular social service.

Virtual Worlds for Kids – Comprehensive review and informational site providing many reviews of virtual worlds of kids.

Yahoo Safely – An online resource filled with articles, tips and insights on how to make smart and safer choices online, as well as advice for using Yahoo! Products in a safe and positive fashion.

YouthSpark Hub – A place to download free educational materials, learn key security terms, watch videos about Internet privacy and security, and check up on the latest Microsoft research on online safety.

ABOUT SCOTT STEINBERG

Bestselling business author Scott Steinberg is one of the world's most celebrated professional speakers, futurists, and strategic innovation consultants, as seen in 600+ outlets from CNN to The Wall St. Journal. The author of Make Change Work for You: 10 Ways to Future-Proof Yourself, Fearlessly Innovate and Succeed Despite Uncertainty, the Fortune 500 calls him a "defining figure in business and technology" and "top trendsetter to follow." An internationally-renowned consumer and business trends expert, Fortune magazine recently named this leading trend forecaster and futurist the "master of innovation."

The CEO of management consulting and market research firm FutureProof Strategies, he helps clients create value and cultivate competitive advantage on the back of emerging innovations and trends. A top-rated provider of keynote speeches, workshops and seminars for Fortune 500 businesses, non-profits, associations and educational institutes, he's partnered with many leading organizations to deliver game-changing leadership, education, and change management programs. As a trusted advisor to the world's biggest and most well-known brands, he's consulted on dozens of innovative products, services, and marketing and social media campaigns.
Among today's most-quoted keynote speakers and trend experts, as seen by over one billion people worldwide, Scott's 10+ year track record for accurately predicting business, consumer and technology trends has made him a fixture in mainstream media. Today's #1-ranked technology expert according to Google, he's been a syndicated columnist on change and innovation for numerous outlets ranging from Fast Company, Inc. and Entrepreneur to Rolling Stone and The Huffington Post. An acclaimed entrepreneur who's built and sold several startups and divisions, recent works include Becoming Essential, The Crowdfunding Bible, Teaching Technology and the award-winning Business Expert's Guidebook. His motivational speeches, leadership seminars and training workshops are renowned for demonstrating thousands how to become more successful and effective in their life and career.
For more, see www.AKeynoteSpeaker.com.

"One of the best gurus on innovation and competitive advantage strategies to accelerate growth."
--European Commission

"If you really want to know about business, you should refer to Scott Steinberg."
--Sir Richard Branson, Virgin Group

Popular Speeches Include

-- Leading with Innovation: How to Future-Proof Yourself + Succeed Going Forward

-- Change Management: Creating a Culture of Innovation

-- Becoming Essential: How to Build & Maintain Competitive Advantage

-- The New Rules of Marketing, PR and Social Media

-- The Relationship Economy - Reinventing Sales and Customer Service

-- Seeing Tomorrow Today: How to Stay Ahead of the Curve

ABOUT JOHNER RIEHL

Johner Riehl is your typical busy dad, juggling multiple work responsibilities and fulfilling family activities in a way that only parenthood can develop. He's worked in the video game industry for almost 20 years as a publicist, writer and reviewer, enjoying stints covering family-friendly games and apps and even hosting a nationally-recognized podcast aimed at new parents about the joys and challenges of parenthood. From Pokemon to parental controls to poopy diapers, Riehl has covered a vast number of digital and real-life parenting issues, which even included seeing his kids rack up hundreds of dollars buying worthless virtual goods. Still, Riehl marvels at the possibilities of the digital generation, and is working to not only be the best hi-tech parent possible, but also encourage others to embrace and educated themselves on the unique opportunities provided to this plugged-in generation.

ADDITIONAL RESOURCES

For more helpful resources, including free eBooks, tip sheets, training guides and videos, please visit us online at **www.AKeynoteSpeaker.com**.

Additional books and training guides by Scott Steinberg include:

• MAKE CHANGE WORK FOR YOU: 10 WAYS TO FUTURE-PROOF YOURSELF, FEARLESSLY INNOVATE, AND SUCCEED DESPITE UNCERTAINTY

• BECOMING ESSENTIAL: BUILDING GROWTH, VALUE AND COMPETITIVE ADVANTAGE THROUGH STRATEGIC INNOVATION

• SOCIAL MEDIA MARKETING AND MANAGEMENT

• CONTENT MARKETING: THE INSIDER SECRETS

• INFLUENCER MARKETING

• CUSTOMER SERVICE IS BROKEN

• PROFESSIONAL SPEAKERS, MEETINGS AND EVENTS MADE SIMPLE

• CROWDFUNDING AND KICKSTARTER: THE ULTIMATE GUIDE

• THE BUSINESS EXPERT'S GUIDEBOOK - #1 Bestseller

• THE CROWDFUNDING BIBLE - #1 Bestseller

• THE MODERN PARENT'S GUIDE: HIGH-TECH PARENTING - #1 Bestseller

• FACEBOOK FOR KIDS AND PARENTS - Bestseller

CPSIA information can be obtained
at www.ICGtesting.com
Printed in the USA
BVOW03s1819180917

495210BV00001B/23/P

9 781387 156306